NEW ZEALAND
UNDER THE SOUTHERN SKY

CRAIG POTTON

Published By
Craig Potton Publishing Ltd

Autumn poplars, Central Otago

Published by: Craig Potton Publishing
98 Vickerman Street, PO Box 555, Nelson, New Zealand

Photography: All photographs by Craig Potton
except for p33 (top) by Kevin Judd, and p52 (bottom left) by Derek Shaw

Text: Introduction by Annie Wheeler, chapter essays and captions by David Chowdhury

Book design : Jo Williams Design

Cover design: Moscow Design

Printed in Hong Kong by Everbest Printing Co Ltd

First published 1993

© Copyright Craig Potton Publishing

ISBN 0-908802-19-6

CONTENTS

The hongi (pressing of noses) completes a traditional
welcome on to Maungarongo marae at Ohakune for Sir
Edmund Hillary, centre, the conqueror of Mt Everest and a
former New Zealand ambassador.

(Left) 'God of the Forest; Tane Mahuta, a giant 1200 year old kauri tree in Waipoua Forest Park, Northland, contrasts with the diminutive native orchid, *Thelymitra venosa* (above) and the fruits of the kiekie vine (below).

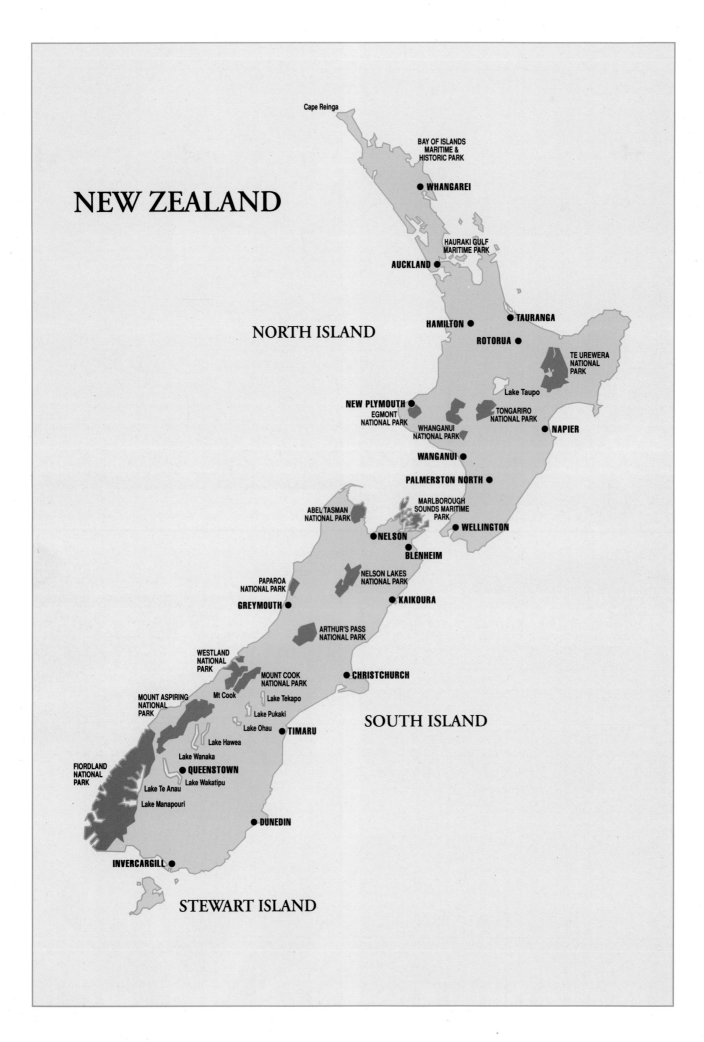

NEW ZEALAND

Cape Reinga

BAY OF ISLANDS
MARITIME &
HISTORIC PARK

● WHANGAREI

HAURAKI GULF
MARITIME PARK

● AUCKLAND

NORTH ISLAND

HAMILTON ●   ● TAURANGA

ROTORUA ●

TE UREWERA
NATIONAL
PARK

Lake Taupo

NEW PLYMOUTH ●
EGMONT
NATIONAL PARK   TONGARIRO
                        NATIONAL PARK
WHANGANUI
NATIONAL PARK   ● NAPIER

WANGANUI ●

PALMERSTON NORTH ●

MARLBOROUGH
SOUNDS MARITIME
PARK

ABEL TASMAN
NATIONAL PARK   ● WELLINGTON

● NELSON

● BLENHEIM

NELSON LAKES
NATIONAL PARK

PAPAROA
NATIONAL PARK

GREYMOUTH ●   ● KAIKOURA

ARTHUR'S PASS
NATIONAL PARK

WESTLAND
NATIONAL
PARK

MOUNT COOK
NATIONAL PARK   ● CHRISTCHURCH

MOUNT ASPIRING
NATIONAL
PARK   Mt Cook

Lake Tekapo

SOUTH ISLAND

Lake Pukaki

Lake Ohau   ● TIMARU

FIORDLAND
NATIONAL
PARK

Lake Hawea

Lake Wanaka

● QUEENSTOWN
Lake Wakatipu

Lake Te Anau

Lake Manapouri

● DUNEDIN

● INVERCARGILL

STEWART ISLAND

INTRODUCTION

Rockhopper penguins on Campbell
Island, 700 km southeast of Bluff.

Long long ago the demigod Maui, using a hook carved from his grandmother's jawbone and his own blood as bait, hauled a giant fish from the Pacific Ocean. It was so heavy that he had to recite a magical chant to help pull it to the surface. He knew in return he would have to make offerings to the gods but his jealous and impatient brothers would not wait and they began to cut and scale the huge fish so that it writhed and thrashed in agony, its flesh becoming jagged and mutilated. At this moment the sun rose; as the rays of light hit the fish it became solid, creating a humped and rugged land.

This, according to one Maori origin myth, was the birth of New Zealand's North Island, called Te Ika a Maui (the fish of Maui). The fish's head is in the south with Wellington harbour as its mouth, and Lake Wairarapa as its eye. Lake Taupo is its pulsing heart, and Northland is its long thrashing tail. Maui's canoe became the South Island, called Te Waka a Maui and the anchor became Stewart Island, which is called Te Puka o te Waka o Maui (the anchor stone of Maui's canoe). The seat of the canoe, which Maui braced himself against as he pulled up the fish, turned into the South Island's Kaikoura ranges, called Te Taumanu a Maui (the canoe thwart of Maui).

Another Maori myth tells of gods who came down from the heavens in a great canoe and travelled so far from their source of power they were unable to return. The canoe eventually capsized and created the South Island. Its giant keel reached up to the sky and formed the high and jagged Southern Alps, while the intricately carved prow shattered and partially sank, becoming the Marlborough Sounds.

European science has since echoed Maori myth in describing New Zealand's origins as a rugged mountainous land, only recently risen from the sea. The Maori people, a Polynesian people of Indo-Asian origins, were the first human inhabitants. Over 1000 years ago they set out from eastern Polynesia in great wooden canoes. The ocean currents and winds and their skill of navigating by the stars carried them in search of the land promised by migrating shining cuckoos and godwits which flew to and from that direction every year. The adventurers discovered an isolated and thickly-forested group of islands that was far bigger than any other in Polynesia. They named their new homeland Aotearoa, (variously translated, most commonly as Land of the Long White Cloud) — the last large land area outside the polar regions to be inhabited.

The first European contact with New Zealand was only 350 years ago. Dutch explorer Abel Tasman was scared off by a disastrous initial contact, and his unfavourable report kept northerners away until the British explorer, James Cook, landed in 1769 and found a pleasant and generally hospitable country. The resulting European settlement began in force only about 200 years ago. Since then the population has grown to about 3.3 million, about 10 per cent identifying as Maori.

It is still a long journey across empty expanses of ocean to reach New Zealand. The two main and many small outlying islands that make up the nation lie isolated in the southwest Pacific. Australia, the closest large land mass apart from Antarctica, is some 2250 km away, South America is 7000 km distant, and Europe 19,000 km. The total land area

Rainforest and limestone gorge, Pororari River, Paparoa National Park.

is about the same as that of Japan or the British Isles. The country is long, 1600 km from north to south, and thin, 450 km at its widest point, so its inhabitants are never far from the sight and sound of the sea. This shape, and the presence of many estuaries and natural harbours, gives New Zealand one of the longest coastlines in the world. However, the land rises steeply from these sea-washed edges and three quarters of the country is over 200m in height, much of it rugged and mountainous. The massive mountain chain of the Southern Alps stretches almost the whole length of the South Island, dividing the island into distinct east and west coasts. The high snow-covered and glaciated mountains rise steeply from the Tasman Sea in the west and spread out in dry plains to the east. The North Island's softer contours include a few small ranges and several volcanic peaks, some of which are still active.

In general the country has a mild, equable, maritime climate, although there are many regional variations and the weather has a distinct unpredictability. It can be hot and sunny one minute, cold and wet the next. Northern regions are at an equivalent latitude to the south of Spain, and Auckland and the northernmost parts enjoy a warm sub-tropical climate, with humid summers, wet springs, and

frost-free winters. Further south the mountainous areas of the central North Island and the Southern Alps experience marked seasonal changes.

The effect of the prevailing westerly wind shows most dramatically on the South Island's West Coast. This region catches furious storms which rise in the Indian Ocean and are borne by the trade winds across Australia and the Tasman Sea before striking the mountain barrier of the Alps. There they shed their wet load in rain and snow, creating an environment of luxuriant forests and low-reaching glaciers. And while the West Coast can all but drown in rain, the east coast conversely experiences long dry summers and many droughts. The far south of the South Island, and more particularly the subantarctic islands, reflect their latitude with cold temperatures and the long summer days and winter nights of polar regions.

The Maori relationship with Aotearoa begins, according to the story of Maui and his brothers, with impatience and acrimony that causes mutilation of the land. Later the European settlers more than matched the demigods' hacking actions with their own drastic use of axe and match, and later of mining and agricultural technologies. The

Southern Alps grandeur: New Zealand's highest summit, Mt Cook (3754m).

settlement and cultivation of this country by Maori and European has resulted in extensive damage to the natural landscape; however, many echoes of the older order remain. There are still times and places where spirit speaks and nature's power is felt, untamed and elemental. This is sometimes manifest in dramatic fashion, in floods and hurricanes, earthquakes and volcanic eruptions, or in more gentle ways, in the rhythms of the sea and the elaborate ecology of a virgin forest.

New Zealand's rugged interior and small population of 3.3 million people, most of whom are crowded into a few North Island cities, means it is relatively easy to find parts of the country left completely to nature's devices. There it is possible to stand and gaze over vast expanses of untouched wilderness of forest and mountain and river, to walk in natural landscape for days without meeting a soul, or to find a deserted beach where there is only the sound of wind and surf and the cry of birds.

THE SHAPING OF THE LAND

Whatu ngarongaro he tangata, toitu he whenua, (man perishes, but the land remains), says a traditional Maori proverb. While this is true from a human perspective, the solidity of the rock beneath our feet is less sure when we look at it on a geological basis. The land follows cycles of growth and dissolution similar to all life forms, only on a scale so vast and slow that we have to step into a radically different time frame to comprehend it. The geological story of New Zealand is one of dramatic interplay between subterranean forces that create new land masses, and the equally powerful forces of erosion that reduce and dismantle those forms.

New Zealand was born out of collisions between large sections, or plates, of the earth's crust. These plates which carry the land masses, continental shelves and ocean floor, float on top of the interior mantle of the earth. A major collision of two, some 500 million years ago, forced the original version of New Zealand up from under the sea's surface, like Maui's fish. The emerging land was made of rocks that had been forming beneath the sea for millions of years.

Summer at St Heliers beach, Auckland, with Rangitoto Island beyond at the entrance to Waitemata harbour.

At this time, the ancient land masses of Australia, Antarctica, Africa and South America were all joined as a single giant southern continent now called Gondwana. Sediment eroded from one edge (now part of Australia) of the supercontinent was compressed in undersea basins to form sandstones and siltstones, and the shells of myriad primitive sea life were similarly compacted to make lime-stones and marble. As well, volcanic material was continually thrown up from under the earth's crust, leaving large masses of granite. Together these rocks form the oldest parts of New Zealand, found today in northwestern and southwestern areas of the South Island. These rocks are as old as 500 million years, making New Zealand seem incredibly old, but the age of these rocks should be contrasted with the 3000 million year old rocks found in western Australia, in what was the heart core of Gondwana.

Weather and the process of erosion ate into the rock around the edges of Gondwana (including what has become New Zealand) until much of the land mass was reclaimed by the sea 250 million years ago. From then, the history of Gondwana is dominated by great masses of sediment which were rafted across the oceans by the moving plates before violently colliding with the supercontinent. Last to be added

were huge submarine fans of greywacke, originally from the granite mountains of South America and Antarctica, about 110 million years ago. Along this youngest collision zone the rocks were metamorphosed to form the great schist belts of Otago and Marlborough.

By now Gondwana was beginning to break up, as underlying plate activity wrenched it apart. New Zealand became a separate archipelago of islands, moving further and further away from its neighbours. This collection of islands was also eroded away steadily until it almost completely disappeared beneath the waves.

The continental crust of which New Zealand now forms a small part has been thrust up out of the sea a number of times during its turbulent geological history. The latest uplift, which began about 25 million years ago, was initiated by the extension of the Indo-Australian and Pacific plate boundary into this crust. New Zealand's location over converging crustal plates also explains the form of the main features of today's landscape. In the South Island the collid-ing plates have thrust up the still-rising Southern Alps. This jagged and snow-covered range of mountains has 223 named peaks higher than 2300m. The country's highest mountain,

Mt Cook, named Aoraki or Aorangi (Cloud Piercer) by Maori, reaches 3754m.

The plates also skew sideways. This has created one of the world's greatest fault lines, the Alpine Fault, which is visible from the air (and even from outer space) as a giant crease running down the western side of the South Island. Many earthquakes have been generated from movement along this fault. Land either side of the fault is slowly being dragged in opposite directions, and rocks that would have lain side by side 20 million years ago are now found 450 km apart in Nelson and Otago. Today the same Nelson rocks are creeping northwards relative to the remainder of the South Island at about 6 mm per year.

Over the last two million years, ice has become a major force in the sculpting of the landscape. There have been series of ice ages each lasting tens of thousands of years during which huge sheets of ice and glacial fingers reached across the land and extended into the sea. Freeze and thaw action on steep slopes shattered surface rock and caused extensive erosion. Several times during this period much of the world's water was locked up in ice. The sea fell to as low as 230m below today's level, exposing a land area that was 25 per cent greater than at present, including a land bridge between the North and South Islands.

The advancing glaciers carved out deep U-shaped valleys and other features characteristic of a glaciated landscape. These can be seen throughout the Southern Alps and, particularly clearly, in Fiordland in the southwest. Enormous loads of rock were carried along with the ice rivers and were later deposited as the glaciers retreated and melted, forming moraines. The great southern lakes of Te Anau, Manapouri, Wakatipu, Ohau, Pukaki and Tekapo are sitting in hollows carved by glacial ice, and the Canterbury Plains are huge outwash gravel fans deposited from the advancing ice. Today, 360 glaciers still extend icy snouts towards the lowlands from the Alps. In the early 1990s these were showing a small advance, but generally over this century they have been on the retreat. The largest remaining is the 30 km long eastward flowing Tasman Glacier, while the two most frequently visited are the Fox and Franz Josef, whose towering terminal ice walls come as low as 300m above the Tasman Sea. Chile is the only other country in the world where glaciers encroach into temperate forest.

(Below) A Maori warrior challenges visitors to the marae.
(Overleaf) A lonely bach on farmland near Puponga at the base of Farewell Spit, northwest Nelson.

Windsculpted dunelands, Te Paki, Northland.

While the processes of uplift, erosion and glaciation have been slowly shaping the South Island over the last few million years, fiery and explosive volcanic forces have been at work in the North Island. Off the east coast, the Pacific plate, buckling under its Indo-Australian counterpart, is subjected to increasing heat and pressure which turn the crust into magma. This magma has burst out through fractures in the crust creating volcanoes, spewing ash over huge distances. Volcanic activity has built the landscape of much of the central and northern North Island including the peaks of Taranaki, Ruapehu, Tongariro and Ngauruhoe. Old craters have filled with water to become Lakes Taupo and Rotorua, the Rotorua geysers shoot boiling water hundreds of metres into the air and there are many places in the central North Island where earth and rivers still steam and bubble; these are all expressions of the powerful forces lurking beneath the surface of the earth.

Even the seemingly placid surface of Lake Taupo hides a number of old volcanic craters that have been responsible for some of the world's largest eruptions. The most recent, in AD186, spread ash over the entire North Island and high into the atmosphere, creating red skies observed from as far away as China and Rome. That eruption is thought to have been at least four times as powerful as the infamous Krakatoa eruption in Indonesia in 1863, which killed 36,000 people in its accompanying tsunami. While many of New Zealand's volcanoes are now dormant symmetrical cones resting in the landscape, others like Ngauruhoe and White Island are still steaming and smoking. Their frequent small eruptions are reminders of the awesome volcanic potential of the central North Island region.

A LIVING MUSEUM OF ANCIENT LIFE

New Zealand broke away from its last Gondwana connection, the Australian land mass, about 70-80 million years ago. When it drifted out on its own into the middle of a stormy ocean, it became a living museum for many ancient life forms. The timing of this separation created an island sanctuary virtually free of large animals, enabling much of the Gondwana heritage to survive in an almost unchanged state. At this point in evolutionary history the great reptiles of the earth were well into their decline and mammals were just beginning to evolve. New Zealand was set adrift with only a few small reptiles — lizards, skinks and geckos, and just one mammal — the bat, of which there were two inconspicuous species. The scarcity of predators meant birds and insects evolved into distinctive and often peculiar forms.

The development of New Zealand's flora and fauna was also affected by radical transformations in habitat. For long intervals the land was mostly covered by the sea. During the ice ages, periods of glaciation alternated with times when average temperatures were much warmer than they are today. Relatively recent volcanic explosions covered much of the North Island with lava and ash. Although many species were undoubtedly lost through these upheavals, especially those adapted to the extremes of hot and cold, many endured by finding small oases in which to survive.

For most of its above-sea history, 80 per cent of New Zealand has been covered with diverse and evergreen forest,

interspersed with areas of mountain land, wetland, grassland, or swamp and coastal dune country. The north of the North Island was dominated by kauri forest, the huge fat-trunked trees often reaching an age of 1000 years or more. Most of the remaining fertile lowland areas of the country were cloaked by a jungle-like temperate rainforest: tall podocarp trees of rimu, kahikatea, matai, miro and totara towered over a canopy of hardwood species, which in turn sheltered an often tangled layer of smaller trees and shrubs and, on the forest floor, a thick carpet of mosses, liverworts and ferns. Numerous climbing plants and perching epiphytes completed these forests.

The most widespread forest type today, beech forests, were well adapted to a wide range of habitats and were found throughout New Zealand. They ranged from tall hard beech which thrived in the lower altitude soils, to the goblin forests of mountain and silver beech which clung to higher slopes. The ancestors of these beech and podocarp forests were covering Gondwana over 100 million years ago, so New Zealand's four species of beech tree share their inheritance with beech species found today in New Guinea, South America and Australia. This commonality is unusual however; New Zealand's long isolation has meant that three

Rainforest enveloped by mosses, Fiordland National Park.

In New Zealand sheep outnumber people by 20 to one.

quarters of its remaining 2000 indigenous flowering plant species are unique to this country.

The dominant inhabitants of the forests were birds. The lack of predator mammals meant non-fliers could survive, such as the kiwi, kakapo, takahe and the now extinct moa. The ostrich-like moa grew up to 4m in height, although some smaller species of moa were about turkey sized. One bird took the usual predator role of large mammals and hunted the moa from the air. This was the now extinct forest-dwelling eagle, a bird so large it would have dwarfed a condor. Other role changes also took place: the niches in the ecology usually occupied by smaller mammals such as mice and rats were in some cases taken by insects. These and other normally small creatures, such as molluscs and reptiles, grew to unusually large sizes. The giant weta is now one of the world's heaviest insects. Several of the 1500 plus species of land snails that inhabited the damp forest floors became enormous by snail standards and carnivorous, with dagger-like teeth. A prehistoric, direct descendant of the dinosaur, the tuatara, has survived in New Zealand's isolated and protected environment. This metre-long dragon, complete with vestigial third eye, has an ancestry that goes back 200 million years.

TANGATA WHENUA -
THE FIRST PEOPLE OF THE LAND

According to legend the first human voyager to visit these wild, bush clad shores was the Polynesian adventurer Kupe. Following his return to Hawaiki, the legendary home-land of the Maori people, there were several waves of migration to New Zealand, beginning around 1200 years ago. The Polynesians brought with them a mythology of a land that was living and peopled with gods, and they developed a culture which wove close connections between human beings and the mysterious and powerful forces of nature and the spirit realm.

In the beginning was Te Kore, the void, and Te Po, the night. Rangi the sky father and Papa the earth mother lay tightly embraced in the darkness and their children, the gods, were clasped between them. The 70 male children longed for freedom and for light, and many of them wanted to kill their parents. But the strongest of them, Tane Mahuta, the father of all living things, intervened and instead used his strength to tear Rangi and Papa apart, heaving his father into the heavens. Papa with her soft curves was the earth, and Rangi, eternally separated from her, wept in sadness. His tears are the dewdrops that form in the night on Papa's back, and make the lakes and rivers; the morning mists are Papa's sighs. Tane was sorry for his mother's grief and nakedness, and clothed her in beauty with his children, the trees. Then he took pity on the desolate Rangi, and gave him the bright sun and silver moon, and stars of light for adornment.

The other gods played in the garden of Tane, each with a special guardianship and role. Rongo-ma-Tane preserved the fertility of growing things of the earth. Haumia-tiketike tended the fernroot. Tangaroa controlled the waves and the creatures of the sea. Tu-matauenga was the god of war. Only one of the brothers had been opposed to the separation of his parents — Tawhiri-matea. He left the shelter of his mother to follow Rangi into the sky where he produced his own children: wind, rain and storms. These he unleashes in anger on the children of Tane, and sometimes he chooses to descend to the earth himself as a hurricane.

The Pohutu Geyser and smaller Prince of Wales Feathers are the main attractions of the Whakarewarewa geothermal area.

Tane Mahuta created the first woman from the earth and slept with her, and so produced a line of god-like men, one of whom was Maui. As well as fishing up the North Island, Maui engaged in such adventure and trickery as trying to capture and tame the sun. It was he who brought fire to the earth.

The earliest settlers of New Zealand are usually referred to as moa hunters. They seem to have been nomadic hunter-gatherers who neither fortified their living places nor had weapons of war. They lived off the then plentiful supplies of bird, fish and shellfish, along with fernroot and other plants gathered from the forest. Large communities were based around moa habitats in the South Island; the huge flightless bird offered a food supply unequalled in size in Polynesia. At some stage, these people developed into an agricultural and warring race, who lived in settled communities. There, the storing of fernroot and cultivation of kumara (sweet potato) and other Pacific Island vegetables like taro, yam and gourds, were essential activities. As the population grew, elaborate earthwork forts called pa were established. Warfare became as common a form of interaction between tribes as the trading of foods or valuable resources such as greenstone (New Zealand jade). Competition for land and resources, or for mana (status and power), fuelled disputes and the tribal nature of the society and the principle of utu (that any act should be repaid equally), meant that feuds were often longstanding.

The land, Papatuanuku, was the earth mother. Mountains, hills, rivers, and lakes were living characters in the myths and legends, and were believed to be the dwelling places of gods and ancestors. Often these features had great mana and were treated with reverential respect — tribes took a sense of belonging from local landforms, which inspired tribal chants, waiata (song poems) and imagery.

The Maori people led a communal life, living in extended families, and belonging to sub-tribes and tribal groups, membership of which was determined by descent from a common ancestor. Economic and social activities were shared and carried out on behalf of the whole community, and land was communally owned. Although title to land might derive from conquest or ancestral right, it was those who lived on and cultivated a piece of land who had the 'rights' to it and were entrusted with its guardianship. Moreover the land belonged not only to those who were living, but was also held in trust for dead ancestors and future generations. To take or use the earth's resources would often necessitate the use of special rituals and prayers, and a rahui (prohibition) was sometimes declared to allow scarce resources to regenerate.

Using the giant kauri, kahikatea and totara trees, the Maori people built dugout canoes and evolved a complex tradition of carving. Meeting houses and other important

buildings and objects in the village were elaborately carved and decorated, often telling the story of tribal heroes or ancestors. Faces were commonly tattooed, detailing the lineage and status of the wearer. Flax was stripped and woven into baskets, wall decorations, rope and fibre for garments. Stone was shaped into tools and weapons, bone became fish hooks, spearheads and ornaments. The ancient knowledge and history was passed from generation to generation through the oral language and in ritual, and was expressed in stories, songs, chants, action dances and movements. This was a sophisticated stone age culture, that developed, like the wildlife and plant communities of New Zealand, unique and distinctive qualities through centuries of isolation.

THE COMING OF THE PAKEHA

The first known European visitor to New Zealand arrived just 350 years ago, in 1642. The Dutch explorer Abel Tasman came looking for the riches of a great southern continent, believed to exist to balance the land mass of Eurasia in the northern hemisphere. Tasman sighted "a land uplifted high", the west coast of the South Island, but after a fatal skirmish with Maori in what is now Golden Bay he returned home without setting foot on land. Aotearoa became a jagged and incomplete line on European maps and gained its European name Nieeuw Zeeland, but Tasman's experience and descriptions did not immediately encourage further adventures.

A century later the great British navigator Captain James Cook circumnavigated New Zealand over three voyages, and completed a remarkably accurate and detailed chart of the coastline. The drawings and descriptions of the hitherto unknown antipodean plants, birds and 'noble savages' that Cook and his scientific entourage took to Europe captured the public imagination. There was also a mercantile interest in these 'newly discovered' southern isles — Cook had noted that the tall kahikatea trees would make excellent spars for the British navy.

The pattern of subsequent colonisation is familiar. First came the traders and hunters, keen to exploit the natural riches of the new country — the timber and flax, the whales and seals. Missionaries soon followed, seeking native souls and concerned about the increasing lawlessness and

immorality of the early trading communities. The indigenous people, who had no concept of race or nationhood before their contact with Europeans, were now acknowledging their identity. They named the new arrivals Pakeha (foreigner) and called themselves Maori (ordinary or normal).

Maori welcomed the muskets and the alcohol brought by the traders, along with their agricultural techniques, literacy and Christianity. However what at first seemed so desirable soon showed its darker side. The introduction of European weapons to traditional Maori hand-to-hand warfare resulted in unprecedented numbers of fatalities. The traders also brought many foreign diseases, against which the Maori people had no immunity and to which their communal lifestyle made them particularly vulnerable. The Maori population declined rapidly.

In 1840 Britain claimed sovereignty of New Zealand as a colony, motivated by a number of factors: the growing number of British residents and the increasing lawlessness of some communities, fears about other nations' colonial interest in the country, the pressure from missionaries and a concern for the Maori people. The result was the Treaty of Waitangi, a document remarkable in that it attempted to gain legal control of New Zealand with the consent of Maori chiefs, by guaranteeing their rights over the country's land, forests and fisheries and purporting to protect their interests. There was no attempt to extinguish or enslave the indigenous people, as had been the approach of colonisers, including Britain, in most other parts of the world.

A flood of European immigrants began. In the main these were resourceful middle class British people seeking a better future than what was offered in nineteenth century industrial England and Europe. They expected a kind of New World utopia, but instead found themselves in alien and rugged surroundings and besieged by land disputes. By 1858 the new settlers outnumbered Maori, who had meanwhile become increasingly reluctant to sell their tribal and ancestral inheritance. For the next 40 years, battles and land wars flared throughout the country as tribes who had not been signatories to the Treaty of Waitangi resisted Pakeha demands, and others discovered fraudulent sales. In the end the colonial powers won out and there was widespread confiscation of land by the new Pakeha government. Today, 150 years since the Treaty guaranteed Maori owners the protection of the Crown, only five percent of their original land remains in Maori ownership. Land disputes are still a source of bitterness and potential hostility between Maori and Pakeha.

(Facing page) South Head, Hokianga harbour, on Northland's west coast.

A HEAVY HUMAN HAND

Since the arrival of humans, the natural world of New Zealand has suffered more decimation than that wrought in the same period by ice, volcanic eruption or earthquake. Maori made extensive use of fire to clear land for agriculture, and much of the lowland forest was levelled to scrub and grassland by uncontrolled burning. Fires, perhaps lit to chase out moa, are believed to have destroyed the forests of Canterbury and Otago. The loss of habitat and heavy hunting took the moa over the edge of extinction, while reducing the range and numbers of many other bird species. The introduction of dogs and rats by Polynesian settlers also had drastic effects on wildlife populations.

When Europeans arrived, their exploitation of whales and seals was so intense that after 25 years the resulting near extinction of seals made sealing uneconomic; in 50 years the whaling industry was virtually exhausted. Kauri forests, their timber much sought after for boat building, were also nearly wiped out. By 1900 some 1.2 million hectares of kauri forest had been reduced to 200,000 ha. Today there is a mere 5000 ha of virgin kauri forest remaining.

A series of gold rushes in the early days of European colonisation saw the sudden rise and fall of mining settlements in the Coromandel peninsula and west and south of the South Island. These left a legacy of abandoned communities along with infertile and often toxic piles of waste tailings.

The New Zealand economy was thereafter firmly built on agricultural development, not mineral resources, but this meant in most cases ruthless development. Early farming methods were characterised by a slash and burn pioneering mentality that continues to plague the country in present times. As the bush was cleared for pasture, timber and urbanisation, New Zealand lost three quarters of the forest that remained when the Europeans first arrived. Swamps were drained and native grasslands grazed, destroy-

Rolling pastures on a Central Otago farm near Queenstown.

(Above) Paddles aloft, the crew of a waka (war canoe) prepare to launch their craft into Auckland harbour during a
Treaty of Waitangi commemorative event in 1990.
(Overleaf) South West Cape, on New Zealand's subantarctic Auckland Islands.

ing more natural habitat. The land's young soils, not long weathered from the parent rocks, were vulnerable when stripped of their forest cover. The soils began to slide away in heavy rains, or needed a continual supply of fertiliser to be productive.

The settlers were pioneers a long way from home — quite literally as far as they could go. They attempted to make their new homeland as much like the mother country as possible through literature and art, and in reality in the way they tackled the landscape. English trees and hedgerows were planted and almost 2000 species of plants introduced, many of them, like gorse, blackberry and briar, becoming serious weeds. Imported rabbits and hares soon bred to plague proportions, and stoats, ferrets and weasels were then brought in to control them. Unfortunately these efficient predators, along with the household cat, have driven a number of native birds to extinction. The introduction of deer, thar, chamois, goats and pigs for European hunting sports has had, and is still having, a disastrous impact on almost all native plant communities.

The colony's early wealth was mainly provided by a substantial export trade in gold, and then in wool, dairy produce and frozen meat, despite the problems and expense of transportation to distant markets in Britain. The transformation of New Zealand into a rich agricultural and exotic tree-growing country was at the expense of much of the indigenous environment. However in the multi-racial society that was developing, New Zealanders began to show more sensitivity as a nation and led the world in several aspects of social reform. New Zealand was the first country to give women the vote, and in the 1930s set up the original welfare state, offering free medicine, free education, a free pension scheme and later a no-fault accident compensation scheme. Increasingly, this sense of justice and equal rights to life was extended to the natural environment. It was expressed in a growing and powerful conservation movement that battled to save native forest, lakes, the coastline and native wildlife. An extensive national park system was created, initially protecting alpine and highcountry areas, and more recently incorporating lowland and coastal habitats. Some three million hectares of wilderness are permanently

safeguarded in 11 national parks and many reserves throughout the country. Conservation attention is now focused on wetland, tussock, marine and other special habitats that remain unprotected, and on the many species of native birds in danger of extinction.

A NEW SENSE OF PLACE IN THE PACIFIC

In recent years, New Zealand has found a new independence and a renewed sense of place as a Pacific nation. The advent of the European Economic Community in the 1970s forced the former colony to seek alternatives to its export ties with Britain. This provided an increased incentive to establish diplomatic and trading relationships with Asian countries. The old economic reliance on agriculture has widened to a diversification of forestry, fishing, horticulture and industry. Tourism is fast becoming a major money earner.

Since the second World War, when America protected New Zealand from the threatened Japanese invasion, and Yankee GIs wooed local hearts, the generally British tone of European Aotearoa society has been affected strongly by the pervasive influence of American mass culture. This is reflected in the highrise city architecture of Auckland and Wellington, in modern art movements, and in popular choice of food and clothing and entertainment.

Auckland's harbour bridge straddles the Waitemata harbour, providing the link between the northern suburbs and downtown Auckland.

In the early 1990s, the welfare state has been all but dismantled, and the New Zealand economy moves into the hands of state owned corporations, self-made entrepreneurs and private companies.

Once a country famous mainly for its landscape beauty and its population of sheep which outnumber humans by 20 to one, New Zealand and New Zealanders are now gaining an international reputation in many fields: art, music, sport, medicine and business. Aside from better known heroes like Sir Edmund Hillary, Kiri Te Kanawa and the All Blacks, New Zealanders in general are known overseas for their friendliness, practicality and ingenuity. Also there is growing admiration for a country that chooses alternative energy sources to nuclear power, and bans all nuclear weapons from its shores, even at risk of provoking the ire of the parental figures Britain and America.

A third and major wave of settlers has come to New Zealand since the 1960s, when Polynesian and Melanesian immigrants from the Cook Islands, Fiji, Samoa, Tonga, Niue and the Tokelau islands began to arrive in increasing numbers. There are now some 100,000 New Zealanders of Pacific Island descent, joining those of Maori descent who number about 10 per cent of the present total population. In the latter part of the twentieth century, Maori activists have been clearly heard vociferously asserting their traditional culture and rights, no longer content to integrate quietly and disappear into what has been an essentially European value system and way of life. Land issues are again a focus of attention, as a legislated review of land sales made under the Treaty of Waitangi (which has also been applied to other resources such as fish) has created a tricky legal and ethical dilemma for the contemporary society.

The Maori tohunga (priests and wise men) carved wood and stone, and the women patterned walls and clothing, with images of the gods and ancestors and symbols that echoed the shapes and forms of nature. New Zealand has inherited an indigenous art that is of the Pacific, and is now appreciating this after long years of European cultural emulation and nostalgia, followed by infatuation for things American. Not only is Polynesian and Maori art still being created in traditional forms; it also influences and inspires

Bungeeeeeee! Taking the plunge above the Kawarau River near Queenstown.

much of the country's recent art. The Maori language and many of the concepts it embodies are woven into poetry, novel and ceremony, as well as being used increasingly in everyday life. Modern and contemporary poets, painters and writers like James K Baxter, Colin McCahon and Keri Hulme have created works that come from a living relationship with the land, its forms, its light, its people and its spirit.

Like many of its artists, New Zealand society has begun to fully acknowledge and celebrate its location in the Pacific, and the dynamism provided by its inheritance of mixed Polynesian and European cultures. The distance and isolation that have influenced the evolution of this country continue to have influence today, but are no longer seen as a hindrance. They provide an opportunity to be distinctive, creative and independent, and to guard the qualities of wilderness that are becoming increasingly rare in other parts of the world.

NELSON · MARLBOROUGH

Nelson and Marlborough have few peers when it comes to comparing attractive lifestyle, pleasant climate and a wide spectrum of coastal and alpine landscapes. Together the two regions occupy the whole of the northern South Island, a landscape that is overtly mountainous in character but which also features fertile plains, across which are spread the 120,000 inhabitants. People relish a slower-paced life in close proximity to bush-fringed mountains and superb coastal areas.

The landscapes of Nelson and Marlborough are easily the most diverse in New Zealand. A cross-section through the region reveals wide geological and climatic variations. Some of the oldest rocks in New Zealand (450 million-year-old granite and gneiss) are found in the wetter, forest clad ranges in northwest Nelson, while some of the youngest rocks (25 million-year-old greywackes and schists) are found in the arid, less vegetated Inland and Seaward Kaikoura ranges in southeastern Marlborough. The mountains of Nelson Lakes National Park mark the northern extent of the Southern Alps, but the Inland Kaikoura range has the area's highest peak, the 2885m Mt Tapuae-o-Uenuku.

A combination of factors has made Nelson and Marlborough landscapes significant strongholds for New Zealand's native plants and animals: the lesser effects of the ice ages on the northern South Island, and the wide range of climatic zones and habitats. A remarkable 65 per cent of New Zealand's 2200 species of surviving native plants are found here and of these, 130 species are endemic to the region. Unique animals such as the tuatara, a living link with the dinosaurs, the Nelson cave spider, Hamilton's frog and the Stephens Island gecko all find refuge here.

The 2500 km coastline is one of the longest of any region. Here rugged boulder beaches on the Kaikoura coast contrast with the low-lying windswept sand dunes of Farewell Spit on Golden Bay's western shores. Between Tasman Bay and Golden Bay lies the revered Abel Tasman National Park coast, where native forests touch the shores and perfect crescent beaches alternate with blocky granite headlands. East from Tasman Bay are the Marlborough Sounds, a weaving 1400 km coastline of drowned river valleys, steep-ridged hills and islands whose waterways are a playground for yachties, fishers and divers. Interspersed along the entire Nelson-Marlborough coast are several significant coastal wetlands and lagoons, including the internationally recognised Farewell Spit, a feeding and breeding ground for an enormous number of migratory and endemic birds.

No less than 40 per cent of the region is protected in recognition of its conservation or wilderness values. Nelson Lakes and Abel Tasman National Parks, and North West Nelson and Mt Richmond Forest Parks are the largest protected areas offering unsurpassed wilderness adventures for experienced, self-reliant trampers.

Human settlement in Nelson and Marlborough began with the Maori who, over 1000 years of occupation, established permanent villages and seasonal camps throughout the region, particularly in food-rich coastal areas like the Marlborough Sounds. Although Maori are fewer in number today, many tribes maintain their sacred and practical affiliations with the landscape. European sealers, whalers and, eventually, settlers followed the explorers Abel Tasman and James Cook and new settlements sprang up in all the major river valleys. Nelson was established in 1842 on the edge of a natural harbour and today is one of the more enduring and pleasant provincial cities. Port Nelson harbours the country's largest fishing fleet while the surrounding rural environment supports a thriving fruit-growing industry and the second largest exotic forest plantation in the country. Across the dividing Richmond ranges, Marlborough's economy, founded on dairy and sheep farming, is now stimulated by a burgeoning wine industry, marine farming and horticulture. In both regions tourism is fast growing, proving a boon for smaller centres such as Picton, Havelock, Kaikoura, Motueka and Takaka.

Immigrants have bolstered and strongly influenced the founding populations of Maori and Europeans. They, along with an eclectic mix of craftspeople, artists, and even housetruck-owning alternative lifestylers, combine to give Nelson and Marlborough a highly visible and fascinating cultural blend.

(Above) Dutchman Eelco Boswijk has served fine coffee in Nelson for over 30 years. His cafe, Chez Eelco, is a city landmark.
(Facing page) The golden sands of Torrent Bay beach in Abel Tasman National Park.

(Above) Forested ridges stagger toward Pelorus Sound, Admiralty Bay and D'Urville Island, at top left, on the edge of Cook Strait. Rising seas since the end of the ice ages have combined with the tilting of the Marlborough Sounds landscape to produce an extraordinary region of drowned valleys and islands. Winds and currents funnelled from Cook Strait frequently churn up seas in the outer sounds but by contrast the inner sounds (left) can be tranquil havens.

Having outlived its dinosaur cousins by 80 million years the tuatara was wiped from the mainland by introduced predators and fires. This ancient egg-laying reptile (above right) is now confined to offshore islands. Stephens Island, an internationally recognised wildlife sanctuary off the northern tip of D'Urville Island, is the tuatara's major New Zealand stronghold.

With their boat moored to a mussel raft (right), a family passes time fishing for cod, while oystercatchers use a buoy as a convenient mid-water roost. As well as being an extremely popular fishing area, the sounds form one of three major mussel farming localities in New Zealand. Fed by nutrient rich waters, mussel spat grow to harvestable size in 12-18 months on lines suspended beneath the buoys.

Until humans arrived, lush coastal rainforest (facing page) such as this pocket in Yncya Bay, Pelorus Sound, was spread throughout the Marlborough Sounds. 'Progress' saw forests disappear to make way for farms. In many areas today, farmland is reverting back to forest, or has been planted with exotic pine plantations.

Marlborough's reputation for wine-making (right) has spread around the world. Blessed with a warm climate and fertile soils, the region has proved ideal for grape-growing. As a result vineyards now spot the alluvial plains of the Wairau valley where once the more traditional industry of sheep farming prevailed. Sheep farming still underpins the Marlborough economy and the undulating Dashwood hills (below), south of the market town of Blenheim, are prime sheep country.

Within a few kilometres of the Kaikoura coast the ocean floor plummets 1600m to the undersea canyons of the Hikurangi Trench. Sperm whales (bottom) feeding on the constant upwelling of nutrients from the trench have spawned a major whalewatching industry here - only a few decades ago along this coast these enormous mammals were hunted down by whalers. Closer to shore the antics of leaping, prancing and diving Dusky dolphins (below) are popular crowd-pleasers. A brooding cloudbank gathers at sunrise over the surf beach at Mangamaunu, north of Kaikoura (right).

Occupying a vast chunk of southern Marlborough's highcountry tussocklands, publicly owned Molesworth Station (top) is New Zealand's largest rural enterprise. An uneasy alliance between profit and preservation exists here - the station's hardy cattle are prized by stockmen, and its conservation values cherished by ecologists. The Clarence River (left) cuts through this region during a typically arid summer on its winding course to the Kaikoura coast. Old ways linger: horses are widely used to muster stock (above) and old cob homesteads dating to last century continue to provide shelter on many of the highcountry runs in this area.

(Facing page) In northwestern Nelson a wind-shorn coprosma (top) staggers away from the constant buffeting of prevailing westerlies on Puponga Farm Park at the base of Farewell Spit. The dune covered spit (bottom) is battered by the Tasman Sea on its northern shore but its protective arm shelters the shallows of Golden Bay to the south.

Internationally recognised as a sanctuary for migratory and endemic birds, Farewell Spit has one of the few mainland gannet colonies (below left). South of the spit, farmland in the Aorere valley (left) encroaches on the forested margins of the huge 350,000 ha North West Nelson Forest Park, easily the most diverse ecological region in New Zealand.

East of Golden Bay, near Nelson, forests of a different ilk, larch (above) and radiata pine, both introduced by humans, form the second largest production plantation in New Zealand - Golden Downs Forest.

Nelson enjoys a well earned reputation as a centre for artists, craftspeople and designers. The vitality and zest of Nelson's creative community is reflected every 18 months in the dazzling 'Nelson Wearable Art Awards' (bottom), an event that turns mainstream fashion on its head. The show is generally regarded as the best in Australasia.

Eclectic architectural styles are also to be found, ranging from the stucco facade of the Golden Bay Lodge (below) and the flower-bedecked garden and lime-washed studio of well known Nelson artist Jane Evans (below right), to the wooden slab huts used by early miners prospecting in Nelson's hinterland (above right).

Low tide exposes mudstone rock formations (below) at the northern end of Nelson city's popular Tahunanui Beach, a safe shallow swimming area and the scene of an annual summer carnival. Yachties find plenty of scope in Tasman Bay and inland on forest fringed Lake Rotoiti (above), in Nelson Lakes National Park.

The undulating Moutere Hills (left), between the lowland plains of the Motueka and Waimea valleys, are covered with vineyards, orchards, pine forests and farms. Wine and new crops like nashi pears have added to the more traditional produce such as wool, shorn by expert and quick shearers (above left).

Rainforests fringe perfect crescent beaches between headlands of granite on the Abel Tasman National Park coast. Not surprisingly, the park's easily traversed coast track which meanders along lovely beaches like that at Pukatea Bay (above) is one of the most popular in the country. Yachties too, find the sheltered coves (facing page, top) of the Abel Tasman coast an irresistible summer destination, while sea kayaking (facing page, bottom) is proving a popular alternative to exploring the park on foot.

Inland forest-lined streams (below right) pour toward the sea, there often merging with tidal estuaries. Granite formations on the coast, including the unusual and aptly named Split Apple Rock (above right) give way to an eerie landscape of water-worn marble in the park's higher reaches, beneath which plunge some of New Zealand's best known cave systems.

From its braided headwaters near Lewis Pass the Maruia River (above) flows through Nelson's southern reaches to eventually merge with the westward coursing Buller River. Snow often closes the Lewis Pass highway (right) that crosses the Southern Alps to link Nelson with Canterbury. The pass marks the southern extent of Nelson's Spenser mountains, most of which are within the Nelson Lakes National Park. (Bottom right) A climber ascends a steep couloir during a spring ascent of Mt Hopeless, one of the more difficult climbs in the park.

(Facing page) The Hundred Acre (or Misery) plateau on the Matiri range, north of Murchison. This striking limestone tableland and its encircling bluffs form just one example of a wide range of unusual karst (or limestone) landscapes that occur in the northwest Nelson region.

WEST COAST

Spanning 600 kilometres from Karamea in the north to the Cascade River in the south, the West Coast region is uncompromising in its abundant mountainous beauty, as well as in its climate. The area's eastern border is dominated by the Southern Alps, an unbroken line of mountains from which glacier tongues creep toward rainforests, and rivers make swift passage towards the Tasman Sea. Waterfalls, lakes, wildlife and a wild coastline complete the catalogue of natural icons which are often startling when encountered. Nowhere else in New Zealand is nature's work so evident.

The 'West Coasters' who occupy the margins of this essentially primeval landscape are easily the most stoic and individualistic of any New Zealand community; on many occasions they have pitted themselves against outside influences in order to preserve lifestyles firmly rooted in their pioneering past.

Although forests on river and coastal plains have been felled for settlement and farming as well as for timber, the West Coast nevertheless remains the least modified area of developed New Zealand. The significance of Westland's landscapes lies not only in their scenic value but also in their importance as ecological sanctuaries. The region's vast podocarp and beech forests and accompanying wildlife are outstanding living representations of primeval lifeforms that existed millions of years ago. As well as providing havens for many endangered or rare species, the West Coast wetlands, and the large areas of kahikatea and rimu forests in particular, are the last of any great size of their kind in New Zealand. No less an august body than the United Nations has bestowed 'World Heritage' status upon South Westland's protected areas, because of their exceptional value as one of the world's great wilderness regions.

Extractive industries - timber, gold, coal and greenstone - and in the last 20 years, the conservation movement, form a huge part of the region's history. For centuries Maori traders traversed the Southern Alps (no easy accomplishment even by modern standards) or came by sea to deal in greenstone won from West Coast rivers. Although the series of gold rushes that began in 1864 saw the local population swell from a few hundred to 30,000 in the space of a year, it was coal mined from seams in the southern Paparoas and on the Buller Plateau north of Westport that would prove the region's most enduring revenue earner. Coal towns like Blackball, Granity, and Denniston, ports at Greymouth and Westport and the transalpine railway across Arthur's Pass were founded and survive on the strength of 'black gold' reserves.

The destruction of West Coast forests inevitably led to clashes between 'greenies' and developers. In the 1970s and 1980s some of the hardest fought conservation battles in New Zealand were acted out over proposals to log north and South Westland lowland forests. The establishment of Paparoa National Park, additions to Westland National Park and the preservation of South Westland forests came about after some lengthy and bruising campaigns. Recently, entrepreneurial West Coasters have turned the region's economic focus away from resource depletion to one in which the appreciation of the region's primeval splendour is paramount. Significantly, tourism now outstrips all of the extractive industries as a revenue earner.

Rain on the West Coast, sometimes lasting for days or months on end, is something of a legend; annual rainfall statistics range from 2000 mm at Westport, 5000 mm at Franz Josef and upwards of 10,000 mm in the high mountains and valleys. But the West Coast can pour on sunshine as well, particularly in late summer and mid-winter. The vigorous climate hasn't put off those drawn by the lifestyle offered. Craftspeople, artists, writers, adventurers, nature lovers and seekers of solitude take their place alongside miners, farmers and hardened old-timers. When citizens get together, it's usually accomplished in the incomparable style of events like the annual Hokitika Wild Foods Festival where it is possible to feast on such delicacies as possum pate, chamois kebabs, goat curry and the ever-traditional feed of whitebait patties.

(Facing page) Beech forest interior, Oparara, north Westland.
(Above) Encrusting lichens and mosses on an old farm gate.

Nikau palms spared from the axe make a stand on a north Westland farm (above). The coastal strip between mountains and the Tasman Sea offered the most promising land for farming along the West Coast. As a result thousands of hectares of coastal forest and its wildlife disappeared. (Left) The ragged forested coastline and bluffs at the mouth of the Heaphy River on the western edge of North West Nelson Forest Park, 15 km north of Karamea. Here the Heaphy track, one of the country's most popular tramps, leaves the coast and plugs inland through forests and open tops to emerge in the Aorere valley, Golden Bay. Northwest Nelson is easily the most diverse ecological area of New Zealand; conservationists have mounted a campaign for national park status, aiming to protect the area from mining and hydro-electric development.

Canoeists drift silently through the Oparara gorge (above) in a region of limestone and dense forests near Karamea on the southwestern edge of Northwest Nelson Forest Park. Caves here contain some of the most important fossil records in New Zealand - opportunities to view such natural wonders are increasing as local entrepreneurs see increasing value in adventure tourism as a balance to the region's long history of resource consumption. (Right) Fur seals in the surf zone of a remote north Westland beach. Almost hunted to extinction, the fur seal is now thriving, especially on the West Coast. Its major threat now is from entanglement in nets of fishing trawlers. (Below) A Karamea dairy farmer and his herd.

A tramper crosses the Fox River in Paparoa National Park (left). The park was created in 1986 after a determined conservation campaign to protect the area's magnificent lowland and coastal forests.

Horses enjoy the last sun of the day on a coastal farm (below left) while a young child wanders knee-deep through foam whipped up by wild seas on a north Westland beach (below).

The Buller valley (bottom) in its lower reaches on the river's westward journey from its headwaters in the Southern Alps.

Wind shorn vegetation (top) including flax and cabbage trees, boulders and an algae-encrusted mudstone shore platform on the Paparoa coast between Westport and Greymouth. At Punakaiki (above) high tide combined with a westerly swell produces spectacular eruptions of water through the blowholes in the layered limestone 'pancake rocks'. Punakaiki is a popular tourist destination and the headquarters for Paparoa National Park. (Left) A coastal walker is dwarfed by an enormous overhang formed by the unrelenting pummelling of the Tasman Sea.

(Overleaf) Erosion patterns in a mudstone shore platform near Seal Island off the Paparoa coast.

The Paparoa range contains a magnificent spectrum of landscapes. Along its crest are jagged granite and gneiss peaks that stand above the forested limestone lowlands of Paparoa National Park (top). Innumerable rivers and streams flow through the forests (above) fashioning enormous chasms, sinkholes, caves and canyons from the water soluble limestone; creeks can often disappear underground into vast cave systems.

Much of the gold won from this area during the 1860s gold rush was found on beaches or ancient marine terraces raised from the sea. Throughout coastal Paparoa, battery stampers similar to this one (left) were used to crush sand in order to extract fine grains of gold mixed with it. A working stamper can be viewed today at Mitchells Gully, 3 km north of Charleston.

In southern Westland, retreating glaciers left a string of lakes in their wake on the coastal plains. In the serene calm of a West Coast evening (left) an angler fishes for trout now stocked in many of these lakes. While partaking of another traditional form of relaxation, a local observes the arrival of a tourist bus at one of the region's better known establishments, the Mahinapua Hotel, a few kilometres south of Hokitika (bottom).

Hokitika (below), population 3300, was established after the onset of the West Coast gold rush in 1864. In 1866 the population peaked between 8000-10,000, with thousands more hopeful diggers, landed by ship at the nearby Hokitika River mouth, camped nearby. In its heyday Hokitika boasted a 1400-seat opera house and 102 hotels. It's a quieter town these days, a centre for government bureaucracies, mining companies, a greenstone industry and crafts.

Few places in the world can boast unmodified wilderness that stretches from mountains to sea. Westland National Park, viewed from Okarito lagoon (top) and Five Mile Bluff (left), joins the highest summits of the Southern Alps across a wilderness of glaciers, pristine forests, lowland lakes and lagoons. Okarito lagoon is the specially preserved breeding and feeding ground of the kotuku or white heron (above).

(Facing page) New Zealand's mountains contain a magnificent array of alpine plants. The Mt Cook buttercup, the world's largest buttercup, flowers in spectacular fashion on a lush alpine herbfield in the Copland valley.

Waters of Okarito lagoon make a swift passage to the Tasman Sea (top) against a backdrop of snow-capped Southern Alps foothills at dusk. (Left) Tree ferns, flaxes and grasses dominate the understorey of this swampy lowland rainforest interior. These forests support a variety of forest birds - including the only populations of the now rare South Island brown kiwi, kaka (a forest parrot) and kakariki (yellow-crowned parakeet). South Westland rainforests contain 14 of the 19 species of podocarp trees found in New Zealand, most notably the dense tall stands of rimu and kahikatea. The kahikatea swamp forests found in South Westland are the last significant remnants of forests once widespread throughout the country, the descendants of an ancient order of trees that existed 200 million years ago.

Three cyclists travel abreast through a forested avenue on State Highway 6 (above).

The Franz Josef glacier, a castellated tongue of ice (left) plunges steeply from alpine snowfields into the temperate rainforest zone. Surging murkily from the glacier's snout is the source of the Waiho River (below) while a little further down the valley lies an emerald green kettle lake formed as the glacier retreated (above). Clown of the mountains, the ubiquitous kea (above left) is the world's only alpine parrot. It is commonly seen near carparks and huts; the golden rule is 'don't feed the kea' because a well-fed parrot has too much time to get up to mischief - often directed towards cars, packs and boots.

(Right) Soaring ice-capped Mt Tasman (3498m), New Zealand's second highest summit, above the crevasses of the upper Fox glacier. The glacier advances more rapidly as it squeezes through a narrow neck of land toward its terminal, contorting surface crevasses into a series of teetering pinnacles (below). On the forested South Westland plains below, Mt Tasman is reflected in tranquil Lake Matheson (above).

(Facing page) Roped for glacier travel, a climber descends the Fox glacier. The Waiho River (above) is still laden with sediment downstream from its source at the end of the other major glacier of the area, the Franz Josef. The spectacular terminal ice walls of both the Fox and the Franz Josef glaciers can be reached easily from the highway and local operators run walking and aerial tours of the ice lands. Wilderness beaches, lowland forests and wetlands of southern Westland (left) 15 km north of Haast and of Ohinemaka (below left), south of Bruce Bay. Tangled rainforest inland of Munro Beach (below) near Haast displays a characteristic understorey of tree ferns with mosses, lichens and vines clinging to the taller trees.
(Above left) Rustic buildings on a Fox valley farm.

Sunset at the mouth of the Cook River (top) where a long sandspit encloses a lagoon and plain of drowned kahikatea trees killed when the river changed course. The Fiordland crested penguin (above) nests in South Westland and Fiordland coastal forests and is regularly seen on beaches near Haast. (Right) Leaves of the aptly named seven finger at Canavans Knob, Franz Josef.

(Facing page) Wetland and forest near Jacobs River (top); Haast River in flood (bottom).

(Overleaf) The huge forested lateral moraine of an ancient glacier encloses Ohinemaka beach and wetland; beyond lie Bruce Bay and Mt Cook and Mt Tasman, New Zealand's highest peaks.

CANTERBURY

Over millions of years, wind, water and ice age glaciers have smoothed the Canterbury landscape, in the process creating the largest expanse of flat land in New Zealand. The Canterbury Plains, today a virtually treeless chequerboard of ordered rural fields, are almost 300 km long and 100 km at their widest. In the west, the plains end abruptly against a line of steeply rising Southern Alps' foothills. This line is broken by a series of immense rolling highcountry tussock basins (the largest being the Mackenzie Basin) in the upper catchments of the region's major river systems. Swiftly flowing braided waterways - including the Rakaia, Rangitata, Waimakariri and the Waitaki - follow paths scoured by ancient glaciers to the plains below where they continue spreading massive amounts of eroded leavings from the Alps.

The backdrop to the area, the Alps, reach their zenith in South Canterbury in Mt Cook National Park, the country's most important assemblage of mountains. It is these mountains whose retreating glaciers have left behind the northern 'great lakes' - Tekapo, Pukaki and Ohau. Substantial peaks, valleys and glaciers stretch as far north as Arthur's Pass National Park. In many places native beech forest intervenes between tussocklands and mountains.

Canterbury's other prominent landscape feature projects into the Pacific Ocean. Banks Peninsula owes its existence to two volcanoes that ceased erupting about five million years ago. Once an island, the peninsula was eventually linked to the mainland by alluvial outpourings from the Alps. Over time the sea has breached the extinct craters of the two volcanoes to form Lyttelton and Akaroa harbours.

The absence of forests in Canterbury dates to early Polynesian settlers who dwelt in large numbers on the coast and on the plains during the 'moa hunter' era. Naturally occurring fires, and those lit to flush the now extinct flightless moa from the forests, were uncompromising in their destruction of vegetation and wildlife. Thus it was that a huge plain of golden tussocklands greeted the first Europeans, filling them with well justified hopes for agriculture. The founders of 'European' Canterbury entertained grand visions of vast grazing runs owned by gentleman farmers, although in practice the plains were more suited to small holdings of mixed cropping and livestock. In fact it was in the foothills and highcountry tussocklands where large sheep runs were created and the gentlemen farmers found the riches they hoped for.

Modern Canterbury is the most populous area in the South Island, with most of its 500,000 inhabitants found in the sprawling environs of Christchurch. The local economy is still based on the wool, meat and crop production of the plains and hill farms around which have grown numerous robust towns and villages. Christchurch is the region's major commercial centre, with an international airport, university, and numerous cultural institutions. Central city parks, oak-lined avenues, the ambling Avon and Heathcote rivers, gothic and Victorian architecture, wealthy private schools, the Anglican cathedral, and even its smog, endow the city with its slightly contrived English character.

Mixed blessings have accrued from the region's climate which regularly demonstrates its extremes. Nothing is quite as pervasive as Canterbury's famous norwester, a hot, dry and dusty wind which is usually heralded by dramatic arches of cumulus over the mountains. This fohn wind sweeps across the plains raising temperatures and testing tempers of town and country folk alike. Norwesters are often followed by chilling southerlies that dump snow on the hills and plains, causing havoc for sheep farmers, and anticipation in the minds of winter sports enthusiasts.

Travellers have long enjoyed a Christchurch stopover on the tourist trail to the mountains, Queenstown and beyond. New Zealanders too, appreciate the region's offerings that range from winter skiing, salmon fishing or journeys into the mountains of Arthur's Pass - all within two hours of Christchurch.

(Facing page) Newly shorn sheep on a Culverden farm,
North Canterbury.
(Above) Grasses, Castle Hill.

Christchurch's provincial government buildings (top) are fine examples of the city's Victorian gothic architecture. They were designed by Benjamin Mountfort who went on to create many Christchurch landmarks including the Arts Centre (above left), formerly the University of Canterbury campus. Christchurch is a major centre for the arts - the city council-sponsored 'Sparks in the Park' concert (above), featuring classical music and fireworks, is a popular event held annually in the 200 ha inner-city Hagley Park.

(Left) Well manicured grass and willow-lined riverbanks, bridges and a punt on the Avon complete a picture of 'Englishness' that the city's founders tried hard to create.

Another Christchurch landmark designed by Benjamin Mountfort is the Anglican cathedral (left), which dominates the city's public heart, Cathedral Square. Three blocks away from the commerce and traffic lies Hagley Park (bottom), set aside by the city's founders as a haven of gardens, riverside walks and sports fields.

On the far side of Christchurch's Port Hills lies Lyttelton harbour (below), an ancient volcanic crater on Banks Peninsula.

Through an ordered patchwork of rural fields the braided Rakaia River (above) channels straight and fast from the Alps to the Pacific Ocean in South Canterbury. With only 500-750 mm of rainfall a year, major irrigation schemes such as the one that diverts water from the Rakaia and Rangitata Rivers are required to sustain crops and livestock. Similarly in North Canterbury the waters of the Waiau River are tapped for irrigation purposes. Acclimatised trout and salmon attract thousands of fishers each year to these rivers.

During high summer the plains are burned golden yellow (left) and shelter belts of pine trees are required for shade and protection from hot gusty norwesters that roll off the Alps. Merino sheep (bottom far left) graze pastureland near Geraldine in South Canterbury. At Waikari (on the route to Lewis Pass in North Canterbury) the Timpendean rock shelter contains New Zealand's best known examples of early Polynesian art (bottom centre). Until fires wiped them out, native forest covered the Canterbury Plains. Today introduced pine trees such as this stand of Corsican pines at Burke Pass (below left) on the edge of the Mackenzie Basin have been planted for shelter belts or for plantations.

The mountains and valleys of Arthur's Pass National Park - ideally located within two hours drive of Christchurch - are a summer and winter playground for Cantabrians. Spurred by gold discoveries on the West Coast the route over Arthur's Pass to the West Coast was pioneered in 1864 and a road constructed by 1866. Although the park's mountains aren't high by Mt Cook standards they nevertheless provide many challenges for aspiring mountaineers. Short walks from Arthur's Pass village, like the excursion to the Devils Punchbowl Falls (facing page) and multi-day tramps, such as the memorable crossing of the Main Divide into the Taramakau valley (above), cater for all visitors to this region. For much of the winter, snow blankets Arthur's Pass, one of the few truly alpine villages in New Zealand. With easy access from Christchurch, its native beech forest surrounds offer rustic settings for holiday baches (left). At Klondyke Corner in the Waimakariri River valley (below left), a low-growing thorny matagouri tree, with its sprawling boughs and divaricating branches, is specially adapted to withstand batterings from wind and floods.

(Overleaf) A thick blanket of snow overlays undulating pastureland near Fairlie in South Canterbury.

South Canterbury landscapes: (top) storm clouds build over crop land on plains south of Timaru; and (above) the rolling green hills of Fairlie, prime inland sheep farming country. Fairlie has a population of almost 900 people and is the major service town for the Mackenzie Basin. (Left) This 'Norman' style lime kiln at Kakahu near Geraldine was built in 1881. Such kilns were used to fire limestone in the production of slaked lime used for building, plastering and fertiliser.

Roads from Timaru and Burke Pass lead into the Mackenzie Basin, a vast area of rolling highcountry tussocklands containing the 'great lakes' - Tekapo, Pukaki and Ohau - that fill trenches left by retreating glaciers. The picturesque State Highway 8 route from Burke Pass to Tekapo (below right) is kept open all year despite snow that covers the basin in winter. A few kilometres past Tekapo, a side road along the shores of Lake Pukaki leads to Mt Cook National Park, a region of glaciers and spectacular ice-capped summits. Beyond the shores of Lake Pukaki stands the massif of Mt Cook (below), the highest mountain in New Zealand. 'Mares tails' or cirrus clouds (bottom) above Lake Tekapo, are a sure indication of approaching bad weather. They are usually accompanied by strengthening norwesters that blast across the basin, buffeting tussocks and trees (right).

Above the boulder-choked Hooker River (left) in Mt Cook National Park, 'hogsback' clouds form over Mt Cook at sunset, heralding the onset of adverse weather. Well worn paths from Mt Cook village lead into the Hooker valley, whose alpine herbfields are bedecked with flowers in summer months. The Mt Cook buttercup (above), a showy member of the ranunculus family, is as significant a feature of the area as the mountain it is named after. It usually flowers in November and January along with mountain daisies, gentians and the prickly spaniard. Walks in the Hooker are among the more accessible in a park which is principally the domain of mountaineers.

(Top) A climber traverses the icy summit ridge of Mt Cook which was first climbed on Christmas day in 1894. With 18 peaks over 3000m, and glaciers covering 40 per cent of its area, Mt Cook National Park is New Zealand's premier alpine region, attracting mountaineers from around the world.

(Above) Hues of pink and red materialise under a brooding sky on the slopes of Mt Sefton (3157m) at sunrise in Mt Cook National Park. South of Mt Cook on State Highway 8, the Lindis Pass (top) marks the divide between Canterbury's Mackenzie Basin and the basin of the upper Clutha in Otago. (Left) A reserve protects one of the least modified Lindis Pass tussocklands. (Above left) A dirt track winds through tussocks and matagouri shrubs toward the snow-capped Benmore range near Omarama.

(Facing page) In sharp contrast with an otherwise predictable tussockland terrain are the striking pinnacles and ravines eroded from clay cliffs in the Ahuriri valley near Omarama.

DEEP SOUTH

While the erosive forces of wind and rain continue to shape Fiordland, Southland and Otago, the greatest influence on the landscape here has been glaciation. Vast pleistocene ice sheets and glaciers have worked relentlessly on the 'deep south', fashioning mountains in the west and planing smooth plateaux and gently undulating basins that extend to the southern and eastern coastlines.

In the mountains of Fiordland the resistant qualities of granites and gneiss have preserved the imprint of glaciation from post-glacial weathering. At 400-450 million years old these are New Zealand's most ancient rocks. Sea-filled U-shaped fiords, sheer walls of rock, and a sequence of glacial lakes - the great 'Southern Lakes'- are dramatic testimony to the work of the ice ages. Fiordland National Park is an enormous wilderness, which encompasses a total of 1.2 million hectares (more than all the other South Island national parks combined), and which is drenched annually by 7000 - 10,000 mm of rain. To the north, Mt Aspiring National Park is almost entirely composed of younger, highly erodable schist rocks that have then been forced eastwards through Central Otago by the obstructing Fiordland mountains.

The westerly fronts that batter Fiordland are usually followed by fast-moving southerly systems that dump snow on the western mountains and rain on coastal plains and pastures in the southeast. In contrast, the rainshadowed tussockland of Central Otago receives as little as 350 mm of rain a year and is affected by extremes of weather ranging from searingly hot summer days to winter hoarfrosts.

Although Maori were more used to subtropical climes, they were drawn to the region by the abundance of the giant flightless bird, the moa, and the treasured greenstone (jade) found on the shores of Lake Wakatipu. Moa were hunted to extinction by Maori, but it is possible the last survivors still roamed Fiordland's wilds when the earliest Europeans ventured into the area. Muttonbirds (a generic term for a range of seabird species) were another important food source, with Stewart Island being the major hunting ground. When Europeans arrived, the Maori population, already reduced

by intertribal wars over greenstone, was confined to small coastal settlements. The Maori community was further reduced by an outbreak of measles brought by the Europeans.

Within decades of Captain Cook sighting and mapping New Zealand's shores, bands of transitory European sealers were busy in the south where they plundered (and almost exterminated) fur seals from all around the southern coastline. In 1806, one shipment alone carried more than 60,000 skins to Sydney furriers. Resolute and hardworking Scots settlers eventually stamped a long-term mark on the south. They sailed into Otago harbour in 1848 and set out to establish major sheep runs in the tussocklands of Otago and Southland. Well used to harsh climates and terrain, the Scots built robust towns like Oamaru and Balclutha and the cities of Invercargill and Dunedin. In May 1861 a Tasmanian prospector struck gold in Central Otago, sparking a gold rush that transformed Otago. Gold towns like St Bathans, Arrowtown and Queenstown were founded. Some of these towns still survive today, while others are merely ghostly remnants, now tourist attractions in themselves. For a time Dunedin became New Zealand's richest city. Examples of Victorian architecture - among them the university, Larnach Castle and Dunedin Railway Station - remain among the country's finest illustrations of the age.

Faced with economic decline in the latter half of this century, the citizens of Otago and Southland have had to work hard to reverse the northward drift of industry and people. Fishing and sheep farming underpin the economy and large industrial developments such as the Bluff aluminium smelter continue to provide jobs. In Central Otago, tourism, centred around Queenstown, has expanded rapidly beyond the traditional attractions of mountains, lakes, famous walks and skiing to encompass a range of adventure activities, historical tours and 'eco' tours. New areas are opening up: more people are discovering the lushly vegetated Catlins Forest Park in the South Island's southeast corner. And across Foveaux Strait, wild and remote Stewart Island is increasingly popular with trampers, sea-kayakers and nature lovers seeking adventure on the edge of the vast Southern Ocean.

(Facing page) A waterfall thunders into Milford Sound in Fiordland National Park.
(Above) A miner's hut, built last century from slabs of Otago schist.

Science has a prosaic explanation for the curious spherical boulders at Moeraki (facing page), half way between Dunedin and Oamaru, but the Maori description of them - the petrified food baskets, gourds and eeltraps that fell overboard from an ancient migratory canoe - extends the imagination. Taiaroa Head on the Otago peninsula (above) guards the entrance to Otago harbour. On its seaward face the headland shelters a world renowned mainland colony of royal albatross.

Otago University's venerable administration block (left) arose in the 1870s during a period of construction in which many of Dunedin's fine examples of gothic Victorian architecture were built. Classical influences are plainly evident in the pillared facades of two Oamaru institutions (bottom left) built of limestone, or 'Oamaru Stone', abundant in the hills of North Otago. The former Bank of New South Wales building at right now houses the North Otago Museum.

A lone cabbage tree 'ti kouka' (right) dominates this rural scene high on Otago peninsula with Otago harbour shimmering beyond. Where the harbour narrows lies Port Chalmers, the region's major container terminal. Overlooking the harbour is the grandiose Larnach Castle (top). Built in 1876 by banker and politician, William Larnach, the lavishly constructed castle has endured changing fortunes that have seen it utilised as both a mental institution and cabaret theatre. At one time in the 1980s an international university was proposed for this stately edifice. Restored in the 1960s, the castle is open for public tours.

St Clair beach (above) is Dunedin's popular surfing and swimming area next to a seaside suburb with the same name.

Rich in wildlife and forest, the spectacular Catlins coast and nearby Catlins Forest Park is little known outside the deep south. A gnarled old rimu tree (top) at Nugget Point is part of the little that survives of the coastal forest that once touched the Pacific Ocean on these shores. Indeed, the forests here are the largest of any on the South Island's east coast. Seals and seabirds are readily encountered along the Catlins' rugged ocean margin, including the yellow-eyed penguin (above), a species becoming increasingly rare on the mainland and considered one of the world's rarer species. Proposals for a marine reserve along the Catlins coast have been floated now for several years. Inland (left) the Purakaunui Falls is the best known of the many waterfalls in the forest park. Forest and coastal walks range from brief five minute explorations to five hour expeditions.

Stoic Scots settlers overcame the bleak Southland climate, infertile alluvial soils and short growing seasons to develop a prosperous farming economy. Near Gore (above) precision ploughing prepares fields for crops of oats, wheat and barley for local and overseas markets. Dairy and sheep farming were established as far inland as Lake Te Anau. While dairying had its heyday in the deep south, sheep (left) were better suited to the climate and terrain.

(Below) A small island in Waituna Lagoon, southeast of Invercargill, is part of a wetland that stretches as far as the Catlins forest and is of international importance for migratory wading birds.

Stewart Island landscapes are amongst the most remote in New Zealand. Increasing numbers of visitors are drawn by its isolation, wild coastline and forest ranges. Magog (facing page), a glaciated granite tor, lies on ranges near Stewart Island's southern cape. Windswept Mason Bay (left) is on the island's west coast.

(Below) A pair of young royal albatross on Campbell Island, the most southerly of New Zealand's islands.

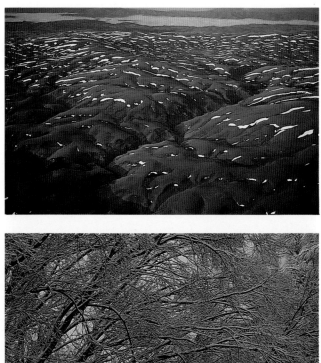

Scenes from Central Otago: The flattened, evenly eroded plateau of the Lammerlaw range (right) typical of inland Otago ranges; hoarfrost holds a roadside forest in its icy grip (below right); State Highway 85 in the Manuherikia valley near Alexandra (bottom); the wind-smoothed clouds of a norwester during sunset over the Dunstan Mountains near Cromwell in the Clutha valley (below).

The St Bathans downs (top) once crawled with thousands of gold diggers during the Otago gold rush in the 1860s. St Bathans is on a side route from State Highway 85 where old gold workings and buildings can be seen, and it's still possible to quench your thirst at the Vulcan Hotel (centre right), the last of 13 hostelries that once served a population of 2000. Goldfield relics also remain at Bendigo (above) one of three ghost towns in close proximity reached from the Lindis Pass road. Central Otago's legendary winter freezes lakes and streams, providing natural rinks for skating and the age-old sport of curling (above right). At Alexandra concrete piers still stand (right) where a suspension bridge built in 1882 crossed the Clutha River. Alexandra is Central Otago's most populous centre and an ideal base from which to explore the goldfields.

(Facing page) Evening shadows steal across the glaciated northern flanks of Mt Aspiring (3027m), a classic alpine horn and the only peak to exceed 3000m outside of Mt Cook National Park. First climbed in 1909, Mt Aspiring is often described as the 'Matterhorn of the south'. It is the centrepiece of Mt Aspiring National Park, a remote 355,000 ha wilderness (the second largest national park in New Zealand) that adjoins Fiordland National Park on its southern boundary. The park encompasses a wide range of territory from the gentler tussock-covered valleys on the east to rugged forested waterways and ranges in the west.

Lake Hawea (above and left) like nearby Lake Wanaka, occupies a trench gouged by ice age glaciers. Its waters are now fed into the Clutha hydro-electric scheme. The Cardrona Hotel (below left), on the Crown range near Wanaka, has survived to continue serving its patrons since its establishment during the Otago gold rush.

Founded in the gold rush, Arrowtown, not far from the shores of Lake Hayes (top), has maintained a rustic flavour with its lovingly preserved old miners' cottages, shops and offices (above right). Arrowtown is at its picturesque best when autumn leaves line streets and the edge of the Arrow River (above). Poplars and sycamores stud farmland near Clyde in the Clutha valley (right). Orchards of apricots and apples have been established in this district but in recent times it has become better known as the location of the Clyde dam, a controversial hydro-electricity project that has flooded the upper Clutha and the original site of Cromwell township.

Central Otago's major tourist centre, Queenstown, is a town of 3600 on the shores of Lake Wakatipu beneath the snowy peaks of the Remarkables (below left). Queenstown wharf (bottom) is the starting point for lake cruises aboard the Earnslaw, a 1912 steamer; for the more adventurous Queenstown is also a base for skiing, bungy jumping and rafting. The popular Routeburn track (top left) begins in the Dart valley at the head of Lake Wakatipu (below).

Lake Te Anau (above) forms a placid entrance-way to the remote mountain hinterland of Fiordland National Park (left). Hard crystalline rock has preserved an ice age legacy of hanging valleys, U-shaped valleys, sheer rock walls and waterfalls. Within its valleys have survived creatures rendered extinct elsewhere. A fine example is the takahe (below) a flightless bird rediscovered in Fiordland in 1948 after it was thought extinct for 50 years.

(Top) Moss cloaks fallen tree trunks in native beech forest on the floor of the Eglinton valley, a tributary to Lake Te Anau and the route to Milford Sound. The Milford road passes through some of New Zealand's most well known and spectacular scenery. Beyond Homer Tunnel a short walk from the road to Chasm Creek is rewarded with views of precipitous glacier-sculpted mountainsides (above). Numerous cascades such as Little Homer Falls (right) are a significant feature of the park.

The sculpting hand of glaciation is dramatically illustrated in Milford Sound (facing page and above). Mitre Peak at left rises sheer almost 1700m from the sea, while the summit of Mt Pembroke (2000m) at right bears the remnant of the enormous glacier that once filled the sound. When the ice ages ended 10,000 years ago, rising seas engulfed this and other valleys to create the park's 14 fiords. A westerly storm (below) lashes the entrance to Milford Sound, sending cascades of water down vertical rock walls to the sea. Many of Fiordland's waterfalls occur only during such storms. No less than 7000-10,000 mm of rain a year is recorded at Milford.

By reputation Fiordland's Milford track (above) is one of the world's finest. Linking spectacular country between Lake Te Anau and Milford Sound, the track negotiates forests and alpine passes, bringing walkers within close range of Sutherland Falls (below) the world's fifth highest waterfall. A small cascade in forest off the track (right) is no less beautiful, as is the view of Mt Elliot from an alpine tarn on Mackinnon Pass (bottom right).

The Fiordland coastline is the most rugged in New Zealand with access from the sea made difficult by constant storms, or if travelling overland on foot, the sheer mountainous nature of the terrain. Doubtful Sound provides a forest and mountain fringed haven for a yacht entering from the Tasman Sea (below). Dusky Sound (left) on the southwest corner of the South Island is Fiordland's largest fiord, with a spidery network of arms and reaches and many islands within its confines. (Above) Alice Falls tumbles from Lake Alice into George Sound.

Vancouver Arm (top) at the head of Breaksea Sound in southwest Fiordland penetrates some 35 km inland from the outer coast. A fishing boat (left) leaves a sheltered fiord mooring for the open coast where gale force winds and mountainous seas like those that batter Puysegur Point (above) are common.

(Facing page) A thick mantle of ferns and mosses carpets the forest floor in the Cleddau valley near Milford (top). North of here rise the highest mountains in Fiordland, Mt Tutoko and Mt Madeline (bottom) on the Darran range, one of the most challenging climbing areas in New Zealand.

FAR NORTH

Northern New Zealand tapers gently to a sandy duneland peninsula where the Tasman Sea and Pacific Ocean roar in unison as they converge off Cape Reinga. Only 10,000 years ago seas surrounding the region were locked in ice. The eastern coastline stretched as far as Great Barrier Island, and the Coromandel peninsula was joined to the main northern land mass. As the ice ages ended, oceans rose to engulf low-lying land, creating bays and gulfs, making islands of volcanoes and high hills, and fashioning harbours from ancient river valleys.

Between Auckland's Manukau harbour and Cape Maria van Diemen, the west coast presents a long and straight edge of beach and duneland. The east coast is more complex, a ragged edge with numerous bays, inlets and estuaries. Both coasts are breached by natural harbours but the west's Hokianga, Kaipara and Manukau harbours impress in the size and intricacy of their waterways that penetrate far into the interior.

Millions of years of volcanic activity in the north has left a distinctive legacy of cones and lava flows that overlays an even older sedimentary landscape. The metropolis of Auckland is constructed on a volcanic field from which more than 50 volcanoes have erupted. None are active today but the nonchalant might remember that Rangitoto Island, the classically proportioned cone opposite the entrance to Waitemata harbour, last erupted about 600 years ago.

Humid summers and wet winters are marks of a subtropical climate - indeed these northern parts enjoy the warmest weather (although not necessarily the sunniest) of all the country. The mangrove-lined estuaries and harbours found throughout the north (and nowhere else) are further evidence of tropical influences. The agreeable climate and once abundant natural resources of fish, shellfish and forests lured early Polynesian settlers, who also found excellent growing conditions for the kumara, yams and taro they brought from their Pacific homelands. The north became one of the most densely settled areas of New Zealand and imprints of Maori habitation are found on most headlands, bays and islands, as well as on the volcanic cones of the Auckland isthmus.

Following patterns typical of European colonisation anywhere in New Zealand, migratory whales, gold and forests around the region were heavily exploited. Discovery of the unsurpassed qualities of kauri for boat building rang the death knell for Northland's enormous kauri forests. Kauri timber and its gum were New Zealand's leading exports for a short time in the 1850s; in just 150 years hundreds of thousands of hectares of ancient kauri forest disappeared, until protests in the 1940s halted the devastation. Reserves in Northland and Coromandel now safeguard the precious remaining stands of kauri forest. Waipoua State Forest south of Hokianga harbour shelters the largest trees, of which Tane Mahuta (51m high, 14m in diameter and 1200 years old) is the highest.

Northland and Auckland remain the most populous regions in New Zealand. 'A thousand suburbs in search of a city' is one description of Auckland, a sprawling metropolis that covers a massive 5200 sq km on either side of the Auckland isthmus. Its one million inhabitants, a third of New Zealand's population, live in nine cities incorporated into a single metropolitan area. The central city highrise of glass and steel houses the country's commercial centre and abuts New Zealand's principal port. Over 10 per cent of Auckland's populace are either Maori or from Pacific Island cultures, making the city the world's largest Polynesian centre.

Balmy summers, beaches and sheltered waters make the north an ocean lover's eden. Nearby Coromandel peninsula and the Waitakere ranges provide plenty of opportunities for trampers, but most Aucklanders and visitors choose to recreate on or by the sea: boating, fishing, diving or living life as an habitual beach dweller. Maritime parks protect coastal reserves and islands in the Hauraki Gulf and Bay of Islands. Amongst these, predator and browser free islands have assumed international significance as sanctuaries for endangered wildlife and plants lost from the mainland.

(Facing page) Boulder beach on Little Barrier Island, Hauraki Gulf.
(Above) Auckland's Twin Towers.

From the narrowing headland of Cape Reinga (top), say the Maori, the dead leap, to be borne by ocean currents to Hawaiki, their spiritual homeland. Once locked in ice, seas have since closed in on the far north peninsula and westward flowing currents have deposited sand to create extensive dunelands like those near Parengarenga harbour (left).

Inland, dunes have been converted to farming and forestry; in particular dairy farming (above) flourishes in the warm, moist far north climate. Slower paced lifestyles suit older ways: a Northland drover is seen here on his trusty workhorse (above left).

Pockets of native vegetation, shrublands, and dunelands (below) near Cape Reinga are part of Te Paki farm park, a scattered 19,000 ha series of reserves. Vegetation in these reserves is the habitat for native wildlife including a rare giant land snail. On the west coast, Ninety Mile Beach (bottom), in fact closer to 90 km in length, stretches southwards toward the hook of Ahipara Bay and the predominantly Maori populated settlement of Ahipara. In earlier times the beach yielded a plentiful and tasty crop of toheroa shellfish but in recent decades such harvesting has been banned until depleted stocks are restored. (Right) A bach at Tauranga Bay, Bay of Islands.

Mangrove swamps proliferate in the tidal reaches of most far north harbours and inlets (right and below) but disappear south of Auckland as semitropical climatic influences dissipate. Mangroves are one of few woody plants able to survive inundation by sea water. Despite the important ecological role these swamps play as feeding and breeding grounds for fish, they are often cleared for land reclamation. A fisherman tries his luck at Houhora harbour (below right) in the company of an egret, an Australian migrant. It took little more than a century to devastate Northland's long-lived kauri forests whose magnificent trees could each 2000 years in age, 55m in height and a girth of 16m. Two reserves south of Hokianga harbour, Waipoua Forest Park and Trounson's Kauri Reserve, protect what is left of a forest that once covered the region. The closely arranged 'Four Sisters' (bottom) are the most revered trees of Trounson's reserve.

Hokianga harbour is a 25 km long ocean inlet whose margins retain reminders of its colonial and Maori history. Farmland surrounds the harbour and encroaches on the beach at the southern headland (top). Rawene (above), is one of numerous small settlements that pepper the landscape. Unlike some 19th century centres, Rawene survived the decline of the kauri timber and gum trade. Old colonial homesteads and churches dot the Rawene harbourside including Clendon House which is open for public viewing. Pakanae (above left) occupies a pleasant rural setting on the harbour's southern edge where the stone used by Maori explorer Kupe to anchor his canoe before he returned to Polynesia is said to be located.

(Left) Boatsheds and moorings on the Wairoa River near Dargaville 60 km south of Hokianga harbour.

Forest cloaked islands, historic buildings, sheltered waters and an agreeable climate contribute to the Bay of Island's popularity with visitors. (Left) While some islands are in private hands most are within the Bay of Island's Maritime Park, a scattered network of coastal reserves open to all. Motuarohia Island's (top) underwater trail, white sand beaches and recreation reserve make it a favoured destination for yachties.

Maori, drawn by the bay's climate and food-rich waters, heavily populated the bay's shores. Rewa's village (above left) near Kerikeri is a superb reconstruction of a pre-European Maori village and is open daily for viewing. (Above) Pohutukawa trees line the flanks of Tauranga Bay on the outer edge of Whangaroa harbour, north of the Bay of Islands.

History abounds in the Bay of Islands. At Waitangi, the lavishly decorated meeting house (top) embodies styles of all major tribes in New Zealand. Near here on February 6, 1840 Maori signed the ambiguously worded Treaty of Waitangi granting sovereignty of their ancestral lands to Britain. Russell lies directly across the bay from Waitangi. For a short time Russell was New Zealand's capital, and before the establishment of Wellington and Auckland, was the nation's most important European centre. Christ Church, built in 1856, is New Zealand's oldest place of worship where gravestones (above) are memorials to colonial settlers, soldiers and whalers. Colonial architecture is well preserved in Russell, including the building that housed the local police station (above right) which dates to 1870. (Right) Marsden Point at the entrance to Whangarei harbour is the location of New Zealand's only oil refinery.

At the foot of the Waitakere ranges the ocean surges against dramatic archways and cliffs north of Piha (left). The west coast is renowned for its surf beaches; nearby Piha beach is a popular summertime resort and year-round surfing mecca. Flanked by Auckland's eastern precincts the Waitakere ranges are a native forest counterpoint to suburbia and glass towers, only half an hour's drive away. As well as sheltering the city from the west wind, the ranges offer drives and walks through forest like this (above) seen from the Karamatua track. At Muriwai, on the coast north of Piha, an angler fishes in a foamy sea from a rock platform (below). Like Piha, Muriwai beach is a favoured summer retreat, a place to swim, fish or gather shellfish.

New Zealand's most populous centre is also known as the City of
Sails - one in 10 Aucklanders owns a boat. A highrise of masts (top)
dwarfs Auckland's downtown tower blocks in this evening view of
Westhaven marina. The city centre is built around the edges of the
Waitemata harbour which is spanned by the 1030m Auckland
Harbour Bridge, the link to northern suburbs (above). At least 50
volcanoes are thought to have exploded on to the Auckland land-
scape and volcanic cones are evident throughout the city and in the
Hauraki Gulf; (left) the Browns Island cone lies off the Tamaki
estuary near the entrance to Waitemata harbour.

Maori and Polynesian peoples comprise over 10 per cent of Auckland's cosmopolitan population since a recent wave of migration to New Zealand has brought settlers from Pacific Islands like Fiji, Tonga, Niue and the Cook Islands. (Right) A festival draws people together at the Otara market. Maori revived ocean-going traditions in 1990, launching waka (war canoes) during the 150th anniversary of the Treaty of Waitangi. (Below) Young warriors guide their intricately decorated waka on Waitemata harbour near Orakei marae. From the air (bottom), downtown Auckland presents a modern cityscape, but Aucklanders have also strived to preserve Victorian buildings like the ferry terminus where daily commuter craft deliver residents from islands in the Hauraki Gulf. Tiny harbourside St Stephens church (below right) was built in 1856 in the distinctive steep-roofed style of architect Frederick Thatcher.

From Little Barrier Island (top) in the Hauraki Gulf a fishing boat is seen plying calm waters in early morning. Gulf waterways are where Aucklanders take to the sea, and are the scene of regattas and races. Waitemata harbour is a waypoint for international events such as the Whitbread Round the World race (above right).

The perfect proportions of Rangitoto Island (above) as seen from Bastion Point, looking across Rangitoto channel. Rangitoto is the most recently active of Auckland's volcanoes, last erupting approximately 600 years ago. (Right) Needles of rock on the northern point of Great Barrier Island.

On mainland New Zealand, habitat destruction and predators have greatly reduced native wildlife populations thus increasing the importance of islands as nature sanctuaries. North Island kaka, a forest parrot (right), seen taking nectar from pohutukawa flowers, and the native wood pigeon (above right) are two species thriving on predator and browser free Little Barrier Island. The island has the greatest range and density of forest birds in New Zealand and is one of the last refuges for gravely endangered birds like the stitchbird, kokako and kakapo. (Below) A crimson flowering pohutukawa tree spreads its branches along the shore of Little Barrier Island; to land here requires special permission from the Department of Conservation. Despite the presence of predators on nearby Great Barrier Island (above), seen here from the summit of Mt Hobson, its valleys and coastline are nevertheless important refuges for wildlife.

Forests of nikau palms such as this one on Great Barrier Island (above) were widespread throughout coastal New Zealand, lending a subtropical element to the landscape. A stream (left) has smoothed and sculpted an old lava flow on the route to Mt Hobson. The island has about 800 residents, and 100 km of tramping tracks for those with an inclination toward exploration. Free from browsing animals such as the possum, Little Barrier Island has the largest unmodified native forest in New Zealand (below).

A decaying kauri dam on Great Barrier Island (right) is testimony to a period of exploitation when most kauri forest on the island was plundered. In recent times some has been replanted here and remaining kauri are now within a forest park. As well as the foresters, miners, kauri gum diggers and farmers exploited the island resources, the latter clearing many hectares of forest in the process. Uses of the petrified gum included burning as fuel by Maori while Europeans rendered it down for high quality varnishes.

Until seas rose at the end of the ice ages, 10,000 years ago, Great Barrier was connected to Coromandel peninsula. The Coromandel has a rugged wooded interior and a bluffed western coast (below) interspersed with 'get away from it all' beaches such as those near the resort of Pauanui (bottom).

CENTRAL NORTH ISLAND

Violent volcanic forces have shattered the central North Island, creating over millennia a complex landscape of extinct, dormant and active volcanoes, and a spectacular region of geothermal activity. This zone of volcanism stretches from Mt Taranaki in the west, to White Island off the Bay of Plenty coast. Collectively it forms an impressive reminder of New Zealand's position on the so-called Pacific Ring of Fire.

It is on the 'volcanic plateau', the region encompassing Tongariro National Park and the Taupo-Rotorua geothermal areas, where the most vigorous indications of the Earth's releases of energy are encountered. Regular eruptions still occur on Mt Ruapehu and Mt Ngauruhoe, and on White Island. In recent memory, volcanic ructions have dealt tragic consequences: the eruption of Mt Tarawera in 1886 and a tragic flood from Mt Ruapehu's crater lake in 1953 each resulted in over 150 deaths. However, these are comparatively quiet incidents when compared with past events that spread volcanic debris far and wide over the North Island.

To the Maori who heavily populated the volcanic plateau, Ruapehu, Ngauruhoe, Tongariro and Taranaki were sacred deities. Their folklore relates how Taranaki fled after losing a battle with Tongariro, (carving a rent through which the Whanganui River now flows) before reaching his final resting place on the west coast. Ngati Tuwharetoa's reverence for the central North Island volcanoes led to their endowment to the nation as a national park in 1887. Until mineral deficiencies in soils were identified, many early pastoralists were defeated on the volcanic plateau. But introduced pine trees, particularly Pinus radiata, flourished. Today the 400,000 ha of production forests north of Taupo are the world's largest afforestation scheme. Forestry has also boosted Tauranga's status as New Zealand's major export port. Fertile Waikato river plains greatly enhanced the development of what is now New Zealand's premier dairy farming area.

For over a century tourists have journeyed to the volcanic plateau to stand in awe before its natural wonders - Lake Taupo, the volcanoes of Tongariro National Park, Mt Tarawera, and Rotorua's geysers, fumaroles, mudpools, bubbling hot springs and silica formations. Geothermal energy has also been put to practical uses including power generation at Wairakei and, as in the city of Rotorua, hot water supplies for homes and businesses.

The Whanganui River, the country's longest navigable waterway, flows through eastern edges of the steeply dissected hinterland between the volcanic plateau and eastern Taranaki. Rich in Maori folklore, history and intriguing scenery, the river begins as a trickle on the flanks of Mt Tongariro and thereafter weaves a 290 km path through beautiful forests and gorges to the Tasman Sea. Maori lived on its banks for 600 years, establishing both a spiritual and practical relationship with it. European missionaries and explorers were followed by tourist laden paddle-steamers, modern day jetboats and recreationalists canoes. Whanganui National Park, created in 1986, protects stands of lowland forest on the river's central and lower reaches where it courses wide and often muddy.

More than 50 rivers radiate from the slopes of Mt Taranaki, an elegant volcano standing aloof in the west above an encircling and undulating ring plain. Its almost perfect symmetry is often compared with Japan's Mt Fuji. Like Fuji, and also Ngauruhoe and Tongariro, Taranaki is a classic andesitic volcano. Five years after it was sighted by Captain Cook in 1770, the mountain belched its last after 120,000 years of activity. However Taranaki is classified as 'dormant' and volcanologists don't rule out the possibility of future activity. Egmont National Park's lower reaches are dominated by forests of kamahi, rimu and rata, the remnants of a huge forest mostly converted to pasture after Europeans moved in. The new settlers discovered terrain made fertile by thousands of years of volcanic fallout; provincial Taranaki's lush pastures have provided wealth for its numerous rural communities, principally from dairy and sheep farming. Discoveries this century of huge reservoirs of natural gas and smaller quantities of oil have added a new economic focus - energy.

(Facing page) First light on the eastern slopes of Ngauruhoe, in the foreground, and Ruapehu.
(Above) Te Tokanganui a noho marae, Te Kuiti.

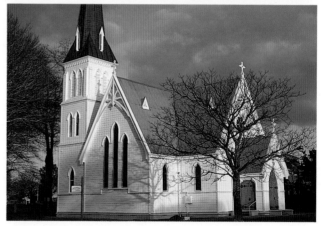

Waikato and King Country occupy the rural heartland between South Auckland and Taranaki. (Facing page) Clad for wet weather, farmers concentrate on bidding during a sale of jersey cattle (above left) at the Taumarunui stockyards. While dairy farming predominates on river plains, sheep suit the large areas of hill country near Raetihi (top). The 425 km Waikato River flows from the volcanic plateau through fertile farmlands to the Tasman Sea. Lake Karapiro (left) is one of seven lakes created on the river for hydro-electric generation. Cambridge is a pleasant rural town 24 km from Hamilton with tree-lined streets and well maintained Victorian buildings such as St Andrews Anglican church (above), built in 1881.

Like spiders attached to a thread, two cavers abseil into the subterranean 'Lost World' cave system (top), part of the remarkable Waitomo limestone region in the King Country. Fortunately there are less daring ways to view the wonders of Waitomo's cave networks, visited by thousands each year on easy guided tours. Impressive galleries of fragile stalactites which have formed over millions of years (above left) and luminous glow worm grottos are readily seen at Waitomo. Above ground, the Marokopa Falls (above) tumble over a limestone layer in forest west of Waitomo. The Marokopa River continues until it reaches the black ironsand of Marokopa Beach (left).

New Zealand's most active volcano, White Island (below right), vents steamily off the Bay of Plenty coast on the northeastern edge of the volcanic plateau. The volcano periodically explodes in a more significant eruption. From gullied deposits of ash flow the outpourings of steaming fumaroles (bottom) towards the collapsed southeastern wall of the volcano's main crater. A visitor has a close encounter with the volcanic forces that power White Island (below). On the mainland, millions of years of volcanic fallout have created fertile land for orchards of kiwifruit near Te Puke (above right) alongside the Bay of Plenty coast.

Lake Rotorua (below right) is one of several ancient water-filled craters in the Rotorua district - among them Lakes Tarawera, Rotoma, Rotoiti and Okataina. In this spectacular geothermal region, roaring geysers like Pohutu (facing page), mud volcanoes, and hot pools have turned Rotorua's surrounds into a world famous tourist destination. The volatility of the volcanic landscape was demonstrated in 1886 when, without warning, Mt Tarawera exploded above Lake Tarawera (bottom) burying nearby villages and killing 150 people. The eruption tore a seven kilometre rent in the mountainside and destroyed the then world-renowned 'pink and white terraces'. Tarawera has been ominously silent ever since.

Maori have always heavily populated the region; traditional arts such as carving (below) are still painstakingly pursued. A women's bowls tournament (above right) at Rotorua reflects the cultural mix now established in the region.

The geothermal wonderland around Rotorua offers treats for the casual visitor and scientist alike, such as the sparkling Champagne Pool at Waiotapu 25 km southeast of Rotorua (bottom). The pool, which has an area of 2000 square metres, was formed some 900 years ago when hydrothermal explosions allowed chloride water to flood the surface; mineral deposits since provide the spectacular colouring. Other marvels include the Craters of the Moon, 5 km north of Taupo (below) and steaming fumaroles and sinter formations at Orakeikorako 30 km northeast of Taupo (right).

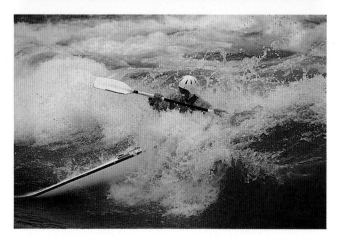

Evening moods on the southern shores of Lake Taupo (top), whose waters fill an ancient crater from which the largest recorded eruption on Earth is thought to have occurred in AD186. Stocked with rainbow trout, the lake and its tributaries are celebrated by fishers worldwide. (Above left) To the south, Tongariro National Park's active volcanoes loom above the lake. North of Taupo, near Wairakei, the Waikato River narrows to a mere 15m before thundering over Huka Falls (above). Only a few brave canoeists tackle Huka Falls, but the Waikato has many 'easier' rapids downstream (left).

(Overleaf) Blue Lake on Mt Tongariro with conical Mt Ngauruhoe and snow streaked Mt Ruapehu beyond.

Midwinter sunrise from the south of Mt Ruapehu's 2797m summit (top) in Tongariro National Park. The shadowed crater lake still steams and occasionally belches gaseous clouds and ash. On Ruapehu's northern slopes (left) snow dapples forest along the Whakapapa River. The distinctive diagonal bark of the mountain cedar or kaikawaka (above) is a feature of forests in the park. Buffered by the Tongariro volcanoes, forests on western and southern aspects of the park survived the great Taupo eruption of AD186 which left a desert on eastern slopes (the Rangipo desert). On the forest floor fungi parasols grow on a mossy tree trunk (above left).

With three ski areas, numerous tramping routes, and climbing on offer it is hardly surprising that Tongariro National Park is one of the most visited destinations in the North Island. Skiers can also chase off-piste challenges, such as on Mt Tongariro (right). (Below) A canoeist takes the plunge over Tawhai Falls near Whakapapa. With parapets glinting in evening sun, Chateau Tongariro (bottom) stands out like a lonely moorland castle on Ruapehu's northern slopes, a luxury destination for the wealthy visitor.

Sheep farming country and scattered remnants of native forest flank the Whanganui River as it flows muddy brown after rain through its lower reaches (left). This is New Zealand's longest navigable waterway; for 600 years Maori canoes plied the river along much of its 290 km course from the mountains of Tongariro to its ocean outlet near present day Wanganui city. Canoes bearing European explorers and missionaries were followed by paddle steamers, jetboats and modern recreationalists' canoes but the construction of a road has ended the area's reliance on the river as a transport route.

Morning mists the Whanganui River valley near Taumarunui in the farmed and finely etched landscape on the river's upper reaches (above). Attempts to farm the mudstone hill country in this region have met with mixed fortunes - many pastoralists walked off the land when terrain stripped of forests slipped into the river. In its middle reaches (far left) virgin and regenerating forests are protected by the Whanganui National Park. A riverbank meeting house in the Whanganui valley (centre left) stands as a reminder of the spiritual and practical relationship established by Maori with the river. Wanganui, a city of 40,000 was established in 1841, one of the earliest settlements in New Zealand's European history. The Sarjeant Art Gallery (left) contains many colonial paintings of the period.

Mt Taranaki (2518m) stands aloof on the North Island's west coast, a dormant volcano whose eroded lava flows and furrowed valleys radiate toward surrounding forests and some of the richest dairy farmland in New Zealand. (Right) Mt Taranaki is the most recent in a chain of volcanoes in the region. North of the mountain is the tussock-covered Pouakai range, the heavily eroded remnants of a volcano that was once similar in height to Taranaki. Sunset turns summit snows pink on southwest slopes (above). Taranaki and the Pouakai range form the backdrop to fertile dairy farmland and the tiny Parihaka settlement (below) on the western Taranaki ring plain. 'Lahar' domes behind Parihaka, the result of volcanic flows that have spread from the mountain during more explosive times, are a feature of this western landscape. At Parihaka, 1500 Christian followers of the Maori leader Te Whiti O Rongomai opposed European efforts to wrest their land from them through 'Gandhi-style' passive resistance. Brute force was eventually used to overwhelm them in 1881.

The imposing bulk of Mt Taranaki seen above suburbs of the district's major centre, New Plymouth (above right). The 198m New Plymouth power station chimney has become a significant skyline feature at the entrance to Port Taranaki where offshore gas and oil rigs are serviced (right).

Strips of native forest along streamways on farmland near Stratford (above) are all that remains of a large forest that covered the undulating ring plain around Mt Taranaki. North of the ring plain the landscape becomes more angular: the coastline at White Cliffs near Tongaporutu displays impressive mudstone formations (top). Further north beyond the settlement of Mokau the corrugated hills of the King Country (facing page) run almost directly to the western coastline.

EAST CAPE - HAWKE'S BAY

East Cape is a remote, mountainous domain given character by its spectacular coastline of bluffs and intimate beaches, its deeply corrugated hill country and a backdrop of forested ranges. At its heart is the Urewera wilderness in the Huiarau range, a brooding, misted hinterland covered in dense forest and steeped in Maori folklore. Further north is the Raukumara range whose seaward ridges fall toward the easternmost extremity of New Zealand's main islands, the East Cape.

Issuing from this angular landscape are a crush of rivers and streams that broaden as they near the coast to form the pockets of flat land which hold most East Cape settlements, including the major centre of Gisborne. Today the region is meagrely populated, its scattered rural communities linked by the tortuous roads that wind around the coast and through the Urewera.

In few other parts of New Zealand have Maori cultural traditions survived as intact as they have done on the East Cape. Notwithstanding that Captain James Cook's first New Zealand landfall was at Poverty Bay in 1769, East Cape's rugged and inaccessible nature made it one of the last regions to be settled by the colonists who followed. Maori, who at times fiercely resisted the new culture, today number over half East Cape's rural population and one third of Gisborne's urban population. Maori have resisted the drift to main centres, and have preferred to live close to their ancestral homelands, ekeing out a life from the land; traditional marae and meeting houses remain the centre of community life.

The Raukumara range, and the Urewera district to the south, are enclaves of enormous spiritual importance to the predominant tribes, Tuhoe and Ngati Porou. Te Urewera National Park (214,000 ha), the largest expanse of native forest left in the North Island, is forever associated with the Tuhoe 'the children of the mist' while Ngati Porou hold allegiance to Mt Hikurangi (1752m), the highest point in the Raukumara range and the highest non-volcanic peak in the North Island. (It is often claimed that Mt Hikurangi is the first place on earth to receive the sun's rays each day.)

The legacy of deforestation on the exposed hill country lining the seaward flanks of these ranges tells another story - one of overwhelming land degradation. With each storm, denuded hillsides of soft, saturated mudstones slip into the valleys, turning rivers dirty brown and periodically triggering floods that inundate lowland communities and farms.

South of the Mahia Peninsula, Hawke's Bay presents a rather different visage with its broad plains, ordered fields, vineyards and large pastoral runs. Prosperity has come to this region from its produce - grains, fruits, vegetables and sheep - activities that were established by monied colonists who quickly saw potential in the land.

Napier and Hastings are the region's two main centres - two cities of about 55,000 situated within 30 minutes drive of each other. Devastated in 1931 by an earthquake that left 256 dead, revitalised seaside Napier has assumed the sobriquet of New Zealand's art deco capital, based on the flamboyant architectural style now prevalent in its streets. The wooded hinterland formed by the Kaweka and Ruahine ranges, a continuation of the North Island's mountainous spine, attracts more than 2000 mm of rain annually, in sharp contrast to the plain's reputation as one of the sunniest and driest areas in the country.

While Hawke's Bay, with its pleasant climate, beaches, wineries and architecture, may appear the more alluring of these two districts, East Cape offers rewards for the patient visitor. Remote villages and lonely pohutukawa-lined beaches along the 340 km coastal route between Opotiki and Gisborne exude a yesteryear character lost from many other areas. The region has developed a reputation for its wine-making and makes much of its historical associations with Captain Cook. And the long journey to the Urewera wilderness and nearby Whirinaki forest is amply compensated by the experience of magnificent podocarp and beech forests - the protected remnants of an ancient natural order that has long since disappeared from the North Island lowlands.

(Facing page) One of the standing figures carved by Tamati Ngakaho in the meeting house on the Porourangi marae, near Ruatoria.
(Above) Wind shorn titoki tree on a Waihau Bay farm south of Tolaga Bay.

East Cape's spectacular coastline of headlands and bluffs is interspersed with intimate pohutukawa-lined beaches. (Top) Looking north into Anaura Bay, rolling surf pounds Marau Point where wind and water have sculpted flutings in the soft rock typical of the East Cape coastline and hinterland terrain. The appropriately titled Gable End Foreland (above right) was named by Captain Cook in 1769 for its resemblance to a house gable. The smoothed cliff is a horizontal layer of rock made up of seabed sediment that has been stood on end by earth movements and then eroded. At Tolaga Bay driftwood piles up on the shore (above) where Cook had his first friendly encounters with Maori. A concrete jetty at the bay is a legacy of the period when sea transport was East Cape's only link with the rest of New Zealand. In Hicks Bay, a settlement on East Cape's northern coast, horses remain an important form of transportation (right).

Unlike many other New Zealand regions, Maori culture and history have remained strong visual and practical elements of East Cape's landscape and lifestyle. At the Whakarua Memorial Hall in Ruatoria (above), carvings by renowned master carver Pine Taiapa recall the gallantry of East Cape's Ngati Porou who lost more men in the two World Wars than any other tribe. Taiapa's accomplished work is found throughout East Cape. (Left) The Maori meeting house and marae at Waipiro, which was once the region's largest settlement and a major port and is now a small farming community. (Overleaf) Kahikatea trees up to 60m tall line the edge of Arahaki Lagoon in Whirinaki Forest Park in western East Cape. Kahikatea was once widespread in New Zealand but isolated large stands, such as this one and those in South Westland, are all that remain of these impressive forests.

Cloaked in dense native forest, Te Urewera National Park is a remote and rugged wilderness region. Its 214,000 ha contain the largest unmodified forest in the North Island. Virgin beech forest surrounds Lake Waikareiti (top), one of a number of lakes found in the park. Panekiri Bluff (above left) towers 610m above Lake Waikaremoana, the largest and most attractive of the park's lakes. A number of short day walks (left) offer pleasant introductions to the Urewera but the three to four day circumnavigation of Lake Waikaremoana is the park's classic walk. (Above) Blechnum ferns and tree ferns line a forested streamway in nearby Whirinaki Forest Park.

The explorer Captain James Cook ended New Zealand's isolation from European influences in 1769 when he stepped ashore at Poverty Bay (right), an act that would eventually shatter the world of Maori. Despite their peaceful intentions Cook and his men were attacked by Maori, a number of whom were killed. On the site of that brief skirmish arose Gisborne city (below right), where today the historical associations with Cook have been maintained. A statue of Cook, adorned in an admiral's uniform he never wore, tops Kaiti Hill in Gisborne (bottom). Settlers felled forests to create farmland in the East Cape (below) but failed to consider the impact of denuded hillsides on easily eroded mudstone hill country, much of which is now slipping into the valleys.

A rainbow forming off the Mahia peninsula (top) is perhaps a sign of the good fortune delivered to settlers of Hawke's Bay whose fertile plains and warm climate differed markedly from neighbouring and inhospitable East Cape. Fine beaches and good fishing distinguish Mahia peninsula (above) at the northern end of Hawke's Bay. Cape Kidnappers (above left), a promontory at the bay's southern extremity southeast of Napier, is the location of New Zealand's largest breeding colony of Australasian gannets which attracts not just gannets but also thousands of tourists a year. Six kilometres from Havelock North, Te Mata peak (left) affords excellent views of Hawke's Bay and the Tukituki valley below. The peak is readily accessible by road.

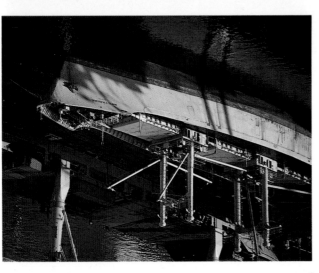

Lake Tutira, 40 km north of Napier, is as much a sanctuary for native birds as for introduced waterfowl like the black swan (left). Thanks to its late owner, the farmer, naturalist and conservationist W. Guthrie Smith, Lake Tutira is now a popular spot for swimming, fishing and walking. By repute Napier's collection of art deco buildings is the finest in the world. The lively 1930s style is typified in buildings such as the Provincial Hotel (below left) and perhaps its most famous symbol, the Rothmans Building (bottom). Hawke's Bay has prospered from wealth generated by market gardens, orchards, sheep and vineyards, produce from which is exported worldwide from Napier's port (below).

LOWER NORTH ISLAND

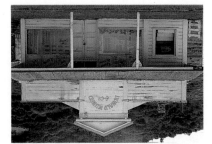

The forested Rimutaka and Tararua ranges are the southernmost expression of the North Island's mountainous spine that has its northern limit at East Cape. Pushed up by activity along an eastern-lying fault, the ranges divide east and western regions of the lower North Island much as the Southern Alps segregate Westland from Canterbury. Set against this hilly backdrop are the fertile plains of Wairarapa on the east, and Manawatu, Horowhenua and the hill suburbs of greater Wellington on the west.

The characteristically rugged west coast rocky shores and cliffs southwest of Wellington eventually give way to long sandy surf beaches that arc northwards as the edge of the South Taranaki Bight. The coastal flood plains of Horowhenua and Manawatu have been cultivated into highly productive market gardens, and into mixed crop and dairy farms that generate sustenance for Wellington city and for export markets. The foothills rising gently against the Tararua range have proved choice sheep farming country. Palmerston North, Manawatu's major urban centre, lies on the northern banks of the Manawatu River, just a few kilometres from the point where the river begins to force its way through a spectacular 16 km gorge between the Tararua and Ruahine ranges.

Wairarapa's landscape is a little more complex, occupying as it does a series of broad plains, basins and hill country between the bluffed Pacific Coast and the ranges. Southern Wairarapa, where large pastoral runs were established by rich Wellington colonists, is the oldest farming region in New Zealand. A series of rural towns sprang up all the way to Hawke's Bay and centres like Dannevirke and Norsewood reflect their Danish and Norwegian founders - tireless workers responsible for clearing large areas of northern Wairarapa forest. The wild and inaccessible Wairarapa coastline runs 350 km between Cape Kidnappers and Cape Palliser, the North Island's southernmost point. The surf beaches at Castlepoint and Riversdale are two locations where one can marvel at the stark natural beauty of this coastline.

Wellington, the nation's capital, has a cosmopolitan population of around 350,000, including concentrations of Pacific, Asian and European ethnic minorities. When combined with neighbouring Porirua and the Hutt valley, Greater Wellington is New Zealand's second largest urban area. It is the country's political and financial centre - the home of Parliament, accompanying government departments, lobbyists and major companies. While some would argue that all of New Zealand is at risk from earthquakes, that risk is acutely felt in Wellington which, unbeknown to its European founders, was built across a major fault line. The threat of a major earthquake has contributed to the transformation of downtown Wellington, which was once redolent with splendid Victorian architecture. Steel and glass now rise against hill suburbs where old villas retain something of the city's original character. The last big earthquake in 1855 raised the seabed two metres, creating much of the flat land central Wellington is now located on, and the shelf that carries the Hutt motorway.

Although the city is bedevilled by its reputation as one of the windiest cities in the world, Wellingtonians merely turn up their collars and seek solace from the elements indoors in any one of its many central city cafes, galleries, bars and ethnic eateries. The city's reputation as a centre for music and the arts has grown in recent years, as demonstrated by its host of mainstream and fringe playhouses, music venues, cinemas and by its cultural highpoint, a biennial international arts festival.

The destruction of wilderness values by forest fires and introduced predators has been no less felt in the lower North Island than in the rest of the country. But Kapiti Island, about five kilometres off Paraparaumu on the Kapiti Coast, has joined the growing list of internationally important island bird sanctuaries. Here, endangered species such as the kiwi, kaka and saddleback, and many other more common species, can survive much as they did for thousands of years before humans arrived. In 1992 a marine reserve was declared off the island's northern tip, extending protection to all sea creatures within its bounds. For good reasons most island sanctuaries are off limits but Kapiti is open for organised tours that offer an opportunity to experience something of primeval New Zealand.

(Facing page) A brass band strikes up at a Wellington festival.

(Above) Mangaweka General Store, Mangaweka.

Central Wellington (above), looking south through Newtown to Island Bay. A statue of wartime Prime Minister Peter Fraser (below) stands opposite Parliament in front of Government Buildings, one of the world's largest wooden structures. While the Victorian heart of downtown Wellington has been overwhelmed by modern glass and steel, wooden terrace houses (left) in hill suburbs retain the city's former character. Oriental Bay's fountain (below left) spurts into life at dawn on the edge of Wellington harbour.

(Below) Yachts moored in Oriental Bay beneath clusters of wooden houses and apartment blocks on Mt Victoria, one of Wellington's hill and harbourside suburbs. Rather than tear down the old wooden terrace houses in the central city, many owners have chosen to refurbish and rejuvenate them, like the example in Tinakori Road (right).

A Lambton Quay mural lends a touch of the ocean to Wellington's busiest shopping street (bottom), an area which in fact was underwater until a 1855 earthquake raised the seabed 2m. The earthquake created much of the flat land central Wellington is now built on, as well as the shelf along the edge of the harbour now accommodating the Hutt highway.

(Top) Sunset on Wellington's exposed southwest coast, a place popular with divers, walkers and mountain-bikers. Pockets of virgin and regenerating forest survive on steep slopes above these windlashed shores. Lake Papaitonga and its surrounding forests near Levin (above) escaped the widespread drainage of wetlands to make way for farming on the Horowhenua Plains. It is now an important sanctuary for birdlife and a pleasant swimming and walking area. (Above right) A Horowhenua dairy farm on the edge of the Tararua ranges. Dunes enclose the surf club buildings at Foxton Beach (right), a resort town popular with swimmers and surfers. This soft duneland coastline sweeps from just north of Wellington to Taranaki along the edge of the South Taranaki Bight.

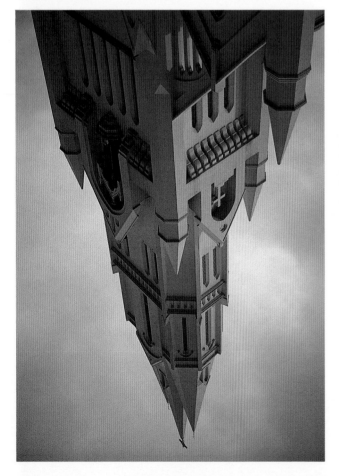

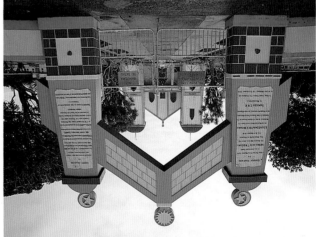

At Ratana, 23 km southeast of Wanganui, this twin-spired temple (below) is the home of the Ratana movement whose adherents are followers of Jehovah. Founded in 1918 by Tahupotiki Wiremu Ratana, the Ratana church has been an influential force in Maori life and politics. Even today the Ratana movement professes to over 30,000 faithful. (Right) The impressive gothic facade of a church in Palmerston North, Manawatu's main centre and the second largest inland city in the North Island. (Bottom) Sunset on State Highway 1 near Bulls on the Rangitikei Plains.

WONDERS
NEVER CEASE

EDINBURGH ZOO INTO THE 21st CENTURY

John Lloyd

Photography
Alan R Thomson

The ABR Company Limited

in association with

The Royal Zoological Society of Scotland

Copyright © The Royal Zoological Society of Scotland
Text © John Lloyd

Published by
The ABR Company Limited
The Barn, Ford Farm, Bradford Leigh, Bradford on Avon, Wiltshire BA15 2RP, United Kingdom

First published in Great Britain 2006

British Library Cataloguing in Publication Data
A CIP catalogue record for this book is available from the British Library

Text by John Lloyd
Edited by Amanda Alabaster
Photography by Alan R Thomson
Publishing consultancy by Allan Brunton-Reed
Design, page layout and cover by Eric Drewery
Endpaper artwork by Graham Catlow
Printed in China by 1010 Printing International Ltd
on behalf of Compass Press Ltd

ISBN 1-904050-13 1

CONTENTS

FOREWORD

Miranda Stevenson

Zoos have an amazing ability to change and refocus, from the menageries of old to modern dynamic conservation centres for the 21st century. Edinburgh Zoo is, and always has been, at the forefront of this change process, from the innovative original designs of Geddes and Mears to the exciting and dynamic plans for the 'new zoo' which will truly be a centre for integrated conservation, from zoo to wild.

People do not always realise how rapid, especially during the last 30 years, this change of focus has been. This book is a wonderful demonstration of this evolution. In the 1950s animals were characters like Philip, the smoking chimp, who probably also took part in tea-parties. Now the zoo's chimps form one of the largest breeding groups in the country and are about to have a wonderful new environment linked to the field conservation project in the Budongo Forest, Uganda.

Edinburgh was at the forefront of the realisation that zoos are unparalleled as resources for education and it is still a global leader of zoo-led conservation education.

It is also important that zoos build on their individual strengths, and the one for which Edinburgh has to be most famous is the penguins. The zoo pioneered breeding techniques for penguins in its early years and continued more recently with the hatching and rearing of king and macaroni penguins in the 1990s, and the opening of the world's largest penguin pool in 1992, once again

Left Chimpanzee (IUCN status: Endangered)

Rockhopper penguin
(IUCN status: Vulnerable)

desert antelope. Scimitar-horned oryx from the zoo, along with those from Marwell and Whipsnade, were the first to go back to Tunisia in the 1980s to start new reintroduction programmes which are still ongoing. Indeed Edinburgh is a leader both in progressing and participating in species management programmes – the method by which zoos ensure that, by working together, they keep self sustaining populations of species. These are managed to ensure maximum genetic diversity which means that, should the need occur, they are suitable for reintroduction programmes.

The World Zoo and Aquarium Conservation Strategy, a new blueprint for zoos in the 21st century, was published in 2005. This focuses on the integrated zoo, that conserves animals in the captive environment, enlightens and motivates the visiting public and links with active conservation programmes in the wild. With this approach zoos are unique: they can inspire, through closeness to the wonders of nature, the next generations, thus creating new conservationists and biologists who care about the natural world.

demonstrating its skill in managing these birds and also ensuring that the new enclosure had plenty of happy penguins. The penguins will continue as a centrepiece of the new Oceans and Wetlands Biome.

Ironically, considering its climate, another of the zoo's strengths has been the breeding of

This book does not just tell the story of Edinburgh Zoo, it tells the story of the evolution of the modern zoo and the ability of the better zoos to become powerful and influential forces for conservation. Through integrated science and effective communication to their many visitors, zoos are in a unique position to achieve conservation success in many different ways. The wonder of zoos.

Dr Miranda Stevenson
Director BIAZA

BIAZA
BRITISH & IRISH ASSOCIATION
OF ZOOS & AQUARIUMS

DEDICATION

For my grandchildren,
that they may truly know that wonders never cease:
Jasmine, Zachary, Lily and Hugo
and
The One Who Is On The Way

ACKNOWLEDGEMENTS

Many people help in the writing of any book, either wittingly or unwittingly. All of the visits I have made to the zoo, whether as an ordinary visitor, as a working member of the RZSS Council or for purposes of direct research have provided material for this publication.

My thanks go to all of the zoo staff and volunteer workers who have given me facts and figures and who have unfailingly passed on some of their own enthusiasms. In addition, individual and group visitors have led me to ask some of the questions I have tried to answer within these pages.

Special thanks must, of course, go to my knowledgeable editor Amanda Alabaster, who provided that wonderful combination of wise words and cake. The book designer, the ever gentle but efficient Eric Drewery has taken my words and Alan R Thomson's brilliant photographs – all taken within Edinburgh Zoo and The Highland Wildlife Park – and bound them into this lovely whole. Our publisher Allan Brunton-Reed is always a quiet and efficient behind-the-scenes man and this project has been no exception.

It is also important that I here acknowledge the work of all of the past directors, staff and Council of the Royal Zoological Society of Scotland, notably Professor Roger J Wheater OBE (director 1972–98) who effected significant change and laid the basis for much of the zoo today. And finally, my thanks are due to the current chief executive, David Windmill who, along with his senior staff, including the Head of Animals, Conservation and Education Iain Valentine, continues to ensure that in Scotland wonders never cease.

THE ZOO EXPERIENCE

Zoos are amongst the world's most popular visitor attractions. Each year around one tenth of the world's population, more than 600 million people, visit a zoo somewhere across the globe. In Britain alone, some 16 million people visit zoos every year, more than attend premiership football matches.

In these multimedia days it is possible to look at animals in full colour moving across our television screens, in the comfort of our own homes. From our armchairs we can observe all forms of animal and plant life with a full commentary that enhances our understanding. Thanks to the brilliant technological advances in the equipment available we can look in the minutest detail or across the broadest scope.

Marvellous books full of colour pictures are regularly being produced, each one adding to the library of images and knowledge available to us.

The world of animals has never been closer. So why visit a zoo to view individual species in a captive state?

International travel is comparatively cheap. Yet even for those of us in the prosperous West, few are privileged enough to travel to exotic places on safari. Perhaps this is why a visit to the zoo is such an attractive proposition.

Here we can see real animals in real habitats, behaving naturally and not edited by the film maker. Here we can truly experience the sounds and even the smells of wild animals – something not yet available through virtual reality.

Running a zoo in the twenty-first century is a complicated business with certain rules understood to be paramount. First and foremost, of course, is the welfare of the animals. But that cannot be all. Why are they there in the first place?

Previous page Asiatic lion (IUCN status: Critically Endangered)

Right Meerkats delighting the visitors

Over the years zoos have had an interesting and varied history. Once merely a place of curiosity they are now seen in quite a different light. Now they are places of conservation, education and research. By far the majority of animal species in the zoo are in managed programmes, because they are, to some extent, threatened in the wild. While not necessarily conscious of it, the general visitor will probably be aware that the fundamental nature and purpose of zoos have changed over the years. No longer are they merely a place of spectacle and display.

Yet they remain places of pilgrimage and education.

Each year more than 600,000 visitors come through the gates of Edinburgh Zoo. Another 60,000 or more drive and walk around the

Above Immersed in the red ruffed lemur enclosure

Highland Wildlife Park. Yes, we are curious. Yes, we do want to see and experience the reality of fascinating and exotic animals that come from far off places. We do want more than that, however.

We have read about the speed with which some of the animals are disappearing from the world. We are aware, thanks to film and television, that wild habitats are increasingly fragmented or lost, usually as a result of the negative impact of humans, whether through hunting, pollution or competition for land and other resources.

We know that looking is not enough. At the beginning of this new millennium, we realise that we must go deeper. We must try to understand the rapidly changing world in which all animals exist. We must consider ways in which we can do our bit to ensure that the human population does not live its life to the detriment of the animal population. Modern zoos are in the forefront of this thinking. They are uniquely placed to raise awareness and influence change. They are often the first to be involved in action that truly can make the world of difference.

They are also a place of refuge for many endangered species. They offer a living gene bank from which we may eventually be able to repopulate an area with the descendants of animals long since driven from the wild. Reintroduction of endangered species is a long and complex process, and is unlikely to happen often, but it is important that such a course of action remains a possibility. Perhaps even more important is the work to ensure that reintroduction just will not be necessary. Work must go on with the end in view of ensuring that animals will be maintained in their wild state in a sustainable natural habitat.

Although in captivity, be sure that the animals in the zoo are, indeed, wild. They may be in enclosures and they may rely on their keepers for all of their regular meals and comforts, but that does not change their nature.

Apart from the animals in the educational presentations, no animal is handled except for veterinary purposes. This is essential, in order to ensure that, as far as possible, they retain their natural behaviours.

Zoos, because of their very nature, have their critics. It is inevitable that there will be many different ways of approaching any problem. Some people consider the keeping of animals in captivity to be anathema. Zookeepers, however, understand the literally vital role that responsible zoos can play in the twenty-first century. They know that through carefully managed programmes of care, research and positive conservation in the field they really can make a difference.

By inviting visitors to enjoy the experience of a walk around the zoo park, or a drive around the Highland estate, experiencing the wonder of living animals, the Society hopes and expects to influence people into positive action on behalf of the animals, both in the zoo and in the wild.

To know is to understand. The zoo has always had a strong educational focus. If we can see an endangered species in a suitable habitat with the animals living enriched and contented lives, then we may be on board for something more. We may be encouraged to look beyond the enclosures and consider why they might be here. It surely is not just for our selfish enjoyment. We have come a long way from the Victorian menageries where animals were displayed as trophies or objects of curiosity.

Right Magnificent Highland bull at the Highland Wildlife Park

Once entranced by the beauty and wonder of the individual animals, we may be encouraged to consider some of the other aspects of the life of a zoo.

We can learn of the worldwide breeding programmes. We can hear of the research that is being carried out that is benefiting the animals' wild counterparts. We can find out about the conservation work going on in other countries, work that involves local communities and their environments.

Worthwhile work of this nature costs money and there is no doubt that visitor entrance fees and cash spent in the gift shops and food outlets make a vital contribution. Other sources of money include charitable donations from individuals and groups and from corporate and trust funds.

How this money is spent is decided in a number of different ways. The Royal Zoological Society of Scotland runs Edinburgh Zoo and its offshoot the Highland Wildlife Park at Kingussie, Inverness-shire. This body has a council made up of men and women who have a number of different and useful interests and expertises. All volunteers, they offer their experience, time and energies to furthering the work through a highly professional staff and a body of volunteer helpers.

The director of the zoo and his senior management team work to an executive committee to ensure the smooth workings of the zoological parks and to further the objects of the Society in regard to its main concerns of animal welfare, education, research and conservation.

It is important work that rarely is 'just a job' for those involved. The zoo park contains a living community of people and animals and remains open every day of the year, including Christmas day.

Everyone employed in the park does his or her bit towards the whole. Each worker, paid or volunteer, has two main aims: to ensure the complete welfare of the animals and to look after the visitor so that

Left Two of the Animal Antics stars

Right Crowned cranes in the aviary of the Maji Mzuri exhibit

the experience gained is of the highest possible quality.

There is a lot that goes into this. Food for the animals has to be grown or acquired, then carefully prepared according to the particular species' needs. The water provided has to be pure and plentiful. The enclosures have to be secure, yet accessible. The habitats for each of the species must be suitable, if not using the exact flora from the animal's native country, then at least replicating it through leaf patterns and general enrichment of the environment. General and specialist veterinary care must be available at all times of the day and night.

For the human visitors there must be an immediate welcome in the car park and at the ticket desk. Most will be there thanks to the work of the marketing department. Then a trip to a clean – and perhaps even an award-winning – lavatory may be necessary. On such a steep site, the provision of a safari trailer is seen by many to be a bonus as they travel to the top of the hill before walking down. The various food outlets in the park all need supplying and staffing, as will the gift shops. The gardens need tending and the paths sweeping. Children, of all ages, need to be educated and inspired by in-house teachers. Nothing is left undone.

Behind all of this there are support staff dealing with the finances, the human resources, membership and development, and the properties and estates.

The eighty-two acre site in Edinburgh and the one hundred and eighty or so acres in Kingussie need constant care to ensure the best possible environment for animals and visitors alike. Everyone is dedicated to ensuring the comfort and happiness of both parties. These

Above Edinburgh Zoo: going in the right direction!

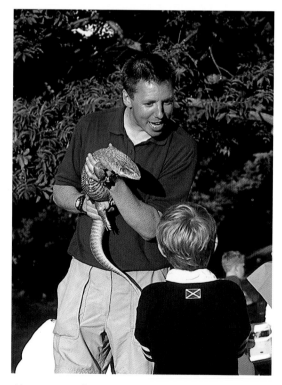

Above Animal encounters, one of the exciting new interactivities

two small communities are part of a much greater whole. The Royal Zoological Society of Scotland has many links throughout the world.

It is an active member of the many national, regional and international organisations that work for the conservation of threatened animal species. The British and Irish Association of Zoos and Aquariums (BIAZA) is based in London; it sets minimum standards, advises on many aspects of animal welfare and husbandry, and supports its members to maintain and improve their programmes of education, training and research. It also works with the government's advisory body, the Zoos Forum, to ensure that zoos in this country are the best they can be. The Society is also a fully committed member of the regional body, the European Association of Zoos and Aquaria (EAZA) and generally participates in its annual fundraising and awareness campaigns. It is also a member of the world body, the World Association of Zoos and Aquariums (WAZA) which strives to improve the standards of zoos around the world and to ensure that the conservation work of zoos is fully integrated into the global conservation networks.

As a member of the World Conservation Union (IUCN), the Society has access to a wealth of scientific data gathered by conservation scientists around the world. All of these affiliations are important for the sharing of information and skills.

Also, through the Conservation Breeding Specialist Group, Edinburgh Zoo holds the studbooks for a number of species. International studbooks are published every two years and European studbooks are updated annually.

Right Gita, Kamlesh and Royal, Asiatic lions in their spacious enclosure

Overleaf Admiring the Eastern bongo

Above Gentoo penguins, a species for which the zoo runs the European studbook

The holder is responsible for the designated population and is required to manage the breeding programme, helping to place individual animals for breeding purposes and ensuring that the best possible genetic mix is achieved and maintained.

Currently members of staff at Edinburgh Zoo hold the international studbook for Diana monkeys. In addition, the European studbooks for Hamlyn's and L'Hoest's monkeys, Pallas' cats, and gentoo and king penguins are administered by senior keepers.

This means that these members of staff at the zoo are responsible for maintaining meticulous records and keeping in touch with all other zoos and safari parks throughout the world that look after that particular species. All breeding is planned to ensure the greatest possible genetic variability is maintained, and that animals are kept in the most appropriate social groups.

When taking on a new groups of animals, it is important to get things right. The keepers have an extensive knowledge of all that is required to ensure suitable and stimulating conditions for the animals in their care, but when new species arrive, help is available from many different sources.

The keeper team will be well prepared when new animals or species arrive. Working with the estates team, a purpose-built enclosure will be properly designed, or an existing one will be redeveloped, in order to create the most natural and appropriate habitat. Through the ever-evolving science of enrichment, keepers will design and furnish enclosures that meet the needs, both physical and psychological, of the animals in their care.

Sometimes senior academics and researchers from around the country will work with the staff, sharing their information and expertise. Many conservation scientists and academics understand the important role for zoos in the work that they and their colleagues do. Veterinary research on drugs and vaccines done in zoos, for example, has been invaluable to *in situ* conservation programmes in the wild.

A modern zoo relies increasingly on partnerships for its work. One exciting partnership at Edinburgh Zoo is with the Scottish Primate Research Group, comprising academics from around Scotland with an interest and expertise in primates. Together they have obtained funding to build an innovative new primate study centre within the zoo, featuring squirrel and capuchin monkeys, that will allow for extensive research programmes that are non-invasive and observational. The research will greatly enhance everyone's knowledge of the behaviour of these fascinating animals and enable developments in the care and conservation of threatened primates in zoos and in the wild.

Under the joint management of the Royal Zoological Society of Scotland and the University of St Andrews, the new centre will provide excellent habitats for the animals, and members of the public will be able to see all that is going on. They will be educated and informed about these species and, in addition, be able to see how good science operates for the benefit of the animal world.

Not only do modern zoos share their knowledge, they also share their animals. For conservation breeding programmes to operate effectively, animals have to be moved around the world, to help form new social and/or breeding groups. As part of the constant development and upgrading of the park, Edinburgh Zoo staff often reorganise the enclosures. So some moves happen within the park itself, but they often require no less planning than moves to other zoos. Animals will be gradually introduced to specially constructed crates and eventually when they can be accommodated without fear they will be encouraged into them for the move. This can be on the back of a lorry for the smaller animals or even using a giant crane that will lift them gently into their newly prepared enclosure.

Those working with the animals almost inevitably have a deep respect for their charges, and they care about them in the widest possible way.

Not all of the work takes place in the zoo. Conservation work can often be best done in the wild – in the animals' natural habitat.

The Royal Zoological Society of Scotland does not just run the zoo and the Highland Wildlife Park. Thanks to money raised from entrance fees and catering and commercial operations, it is able to fund much important conservation work overseas.

Animals in danger

The World Conservation Union (IUCN), based in Switzerland, monitors the situation of animals in the wild and regularly produces a 'Red List' of threatened species. Drawing together information from 10,000 scientists throughout the world, it describes the current status of the various species and identifies the nature of the threat they face. Some are already extinct in the wild and are known only to survive in captivity or in naturalised groups well outside of their natural range. Others are shown to be endangered to various extents, with categories ranging from the designation 'critically endangered' to 'near threatened' or 'vulnerable'. The Red List helps to inform and direct the management of international conservation programmes to save threatened species.

Using both the 1994 and 2001 definitions, the IUCN threat categories can be summarised as:

- Extinct in the Wild – known only to survive in captivity or in naturalised groups well outside of their natural range
- Critically Endangered – facing an almost immediate and extremely high risk of extinction in the wild
- Endangered – facing a very high risk of extinction in the wild in the near future
- Vulnerable – facing the risk of extinction in the wild in the medium-term future
- Lower Risk/Conservation Dependent – dependent on conservation measures in order to avoid joining any one of the other categories, with concern about their ability to survive in the wild without help
- Near Threatened – close to qualifying for a threatened category in the near future

See www.iucn.org and www.iucnredlist.org for further information.

In most cases, species which appear in this book have their current conservation status given as an IUCN category. Where there is none given, this is because the species is not listed in the IUCN list of threatened species. This may be because the species is commonly found in the wild, or because there is insufficient data on which to make an assessment.

It is now understood that one of the greatest threats to an animal species is competition with local communities – sometimes this can include hunting for meat or for the pet trade, but it can even include competition for water where there is a need to provide both for the community's livestock and crop irrigation as well as for everyday domestic use. The zoo's education work with local partners can take in such things as sustainable water management schemes, firearms control and eco-tourism initiatives, all of which might be needed to help preserve the habitat of the animals, at the same time as supporting the economic and social structures of the local communities.

It is reckoned that *in situ* conservation work is seventy per cent about people and thirty per cent about the animals. There has to be a co-operative effort, for people all over the world will benefit from the maintenance of the delicate natural balance on which we all rely.

It is, indeed, vital work.

Occasionally individual keepers will be sent out to work with conservation projects in the wild. After a few months spent in another country observing and working with a wild population, they return with renewed energy to care for the zoo population of animals. All parties benefit hugely from such exchanges.

Back home, Edinburgh Zoo offers one of the most naturally beautiful zoo sites in the world. On the hillside so close to the centre of the city, the animals can live not, for the most part, behind bars as was the case in the past, but in enclosures that include the optimum space and accommodation for the numbers of individuals necessary for natural courtship, reproductive behaviour, the rearing of young and other natural behaviours.

Each of the enclosures offers what is necessary and desirable to allow the animals to engage in natural activities such as climbing, swimming, burrowing, playing and exploring.

By presenting such well thought-out animal facilities to the general public, the zoo staff hope to engage the visitor and encourage a real concern about the animals both in the zoo and in their wild state. Truly these animals can be seen as ambassadors, raising public awareness about the urgent need for conservation of the wild populations and their habitats.

Increasingly, conservationists understand that habitats are crucial to the survival of animal species. Within the zoo there is a rich horticultural tradition which reflects this concern and also provides for a pleasant environment for the visitor. Tended lovingly over many generations, it has some 120 tree species, and boasts one of the most diverse tree collections in the region. In addition, it has 53 species of plant with animal names, including a tree variety called 'Flamingo', a rhododendron 'Polar Bear' and a rose named 'Grouse'.

A discipline in its own right, horticulture in the zoo focuses on the creation of habitats within the enclosures, providing foodstuffs for the animals and offering an enriching environment for both the animals and the visiting public. Throughout the year the gardeners aim to provide displays that will continually delight all who walk around the park.

In the Highlands a different, but equally well thought-out, management scheme is in place for the wilder and more open setting found within the Cairngorms National Park.

Edinburgh Zoo and the Highland Wildlife Park are places where nothing stands still. At all times of the day and night events are taking place, while animals live their various and fascinating lives. The visitor can get a glimpse of some of these, and share in a sense of wonder about the 200 or so types of animal found within the two sites. Here, wonders never cease . . .

BEGINNINGS

In the early years of the twentieth century an Edinburgh lawyer, by his own account, 'became obsessed with the idea of bringing about the establishment of a Zoological Garden or Park' in the city. Thomas Gillespie's obsession and vision was not wasted and it is to him and a few friends that we owe the founding of what eventually became The Royal Zoological Society of Scotland, which body then set up the zoo.

There had been a zoo in Edinburgh that lasted only eighteen years from its establishment in 1839, in the north of the city, not far from the botanical gardens. It appears to have been a popular place that achieved Royal patronage, enabling it to style itself The Royal Edinburgh Zoological Gardens. With an impressive range of 'healthy animals' the zoo, according to its guidebook, was a place 'in which the works of the Great Creator may be studied "in their habits as they live"'. It seems that its demise came about when the zoo was sold off to a commercial concern that was more interested in making money than caring properly for the animals and the original objects

of the establishment. Thomas Gillespie's aims were loftier and, approaching friends and potentially interested parties in 1908, he was initially disappointed with the lukewarm response to his proposal. Eventually, however, enough enthusiasts were mustered to set up a meeting to discuss the formation of a zoological society with the purpose of 'establishing and maintaining a national zoological park or garden at Edinburgh'. Even this was not an immediate success and the meeting agreed to a course of action that entailed the setting up of a small committee to approach the local council and other potentially interested bodies on the subject.

All of this must have been very frustrating to a man of energy and vision, but Gillespie persevered and eventually, in March 1909, the Zoological Society was formed and he became its first honorary secretary. Its objects were defined then as being 'to advance the study of zoology and foster and develop among people an interest in and knowledge of animal life and for these purposes to establish and carry on living zoological collections in Scotland'.

Previous page The Mansion House at the heart of Edinburgh Zoo

Below Edinburgh's first zoo, near East Claremont Street, 1839–1857

Nearly one hundred years later these early goals have developed and are summed up in the Society's mission statement 'to inspire and excite our visitors with the wonder of living animals, and so to promote the conservation of threatened species and habitats'.

Between these two statements much has happened and many changes in attitude and practice have taken place.

Growth of membership of the newly formed Society was initially slow and it quickly became apparent that the setting up of a zoo would be no easy matter. A series of popular lectures was planned and Professor Arthur Thomson gave the first one under the title 'The Modern Zoo'. It included the use of a number of lantern slides and, a novelty in those days, a cinematographic film of the Animal Park run by a Carl Hagenbeck in Hamburg, Germany.

The lecture was a huge success. It was presided over by a Judge of the Court of Session, Lord Salvesen, who made a forceful appeal on behalf of the Society and its zoo project. Such was the impression he made that he quickly found himself elected the first honorary president.

Artist's impression and ground plan of the Carnegie Aquarium, opened in 1927

Press reports of the meetings, lectures and annual reports did much to bring the prime object of the establishment of a zoo to public attention. This publicity led to the family of Francis Ranken, the former managing director of the old zoo, to offering the balance of money left on its closure. Other money was donated and, after a long search for somewhere suitable to establish a zoo, the estate of Corstorphine Hill House was identified. It was offered to the Society in the summer of 1912 at the cost of £17,000. The Society's council decided that a further £8,000 would be needed for the laying out and stocking of the zoo and an appeal for extra funds was launched. Again Thomas Gillespie noted a distinct lack of enthusiasm for the project.

Dogged as ever, however, he and the Society's newly-formed council worked hard to achieve their end and eventually, in early 1913, decided to ask the City Council for direct help. Much to everyone's surprise and delight this was immediately forthcoming and the community leaders agreed to purchase the estate and feu it to the Society. There were only two of the Society's council members who refused to vote for the plan and interestingly – in the light of the Society's distinguished success in education – one of them was the chairman of the education committee.

Now seen as one of the city's most important places of education, his successors in the post must find his negative attitude decidedly strange.

The monarch and his court did not share the education chairman's concerns and in July 1913 the Privy Council granted a Royal Charter. Thus the newly approved Zoological Society for Scotland was felt, in the spirit of the times, to be truly open for business. The prefix 'Royal' was granted in 1948 following a visit of King George VI, and it remains the only zoological society in the United Kingdom with the 'Royal' status.

Thomas Gillespie had been appointed to the post of director of the zoological park and so the stage was set for realising the grand project. There was a park, but where were the animals to come from?

In order to secure an early opening of the zoo, the bulk of the animals came on a three-month loan from Mr Garrard Tyrwhitt-Drake's private collection in Maidstone, Kent. The Society was responsible only for the cost of transport, so had money to spend on beginning its own collection. The first animal at Edinburgh Zoo was a gannet that cost the equivalent of eight pence. It is because of this that the bird is enshrined on the Society's badge.

Frantic work took place to prepare enclosures and cages for the animals. From the beginning and thanks to the superb qualities of the chosen site, it was the intention to display the animals in as open and natural way as possible, taking much from the example of Herr Hagenbeck's zoo in Hamburg.

The animals came up to Scotland in two large parcel vans that were attached to the local train and shunted to Corstorphine station from which lorries were loaded and an early morning procession took place, with two camels bringing up the rear. All of the animals had been unboxed by evening after an eventful day that ended with the escape and quick recapture of a wolf.

For a few days, work on the grounds and enclosures continued with just fellows of the Society allowed in to visit. Then on 22 July 1913 the Edinburgh Zoological Park opened to the public. They came in large numbers and the success of the venture seemed assured. The rush to open proved sensible, as had it been delayed for a year – as was mooted by some of the more cautious members of council – an onward rush into war may well have sunk the project before it could begin.

The famous social visionary and town planner Patrick Geddes, along with his son-in-law Frank Mears, was responsible for the main design of the new zoo. With his known concern for careful planning for humans it is no surprise that his revolutionary designs on behalf of the animal population were quickly appreciated for the free and open environments that he created.

Not for Edinburgh was the old Victorian-style menagerie of bars and cages. Both the animals and their visitors were to benefit from the very best thinking, planning and building. Large open enclosures using ditches and moats to separate the animals from the visitor were used and, as others came up with even better designs and materials, these were incorporated.

Edinburgh Zoo has remained in the forefront of animal enclosure design and over the years has won many awards for the natural and stimulating habitats. Never have things remained static, but at the beginning of the twenty-first century, and nearly one hundred years on from its foundation, great new development plans are coming into effect.

The zoo at Edinburgh became world famous quite early in its history thanks to another animal that appears on its badge and logo. Family links between the president and the Christian Salvesen whaling company brought three king penguins from the South Atlantic to the zoo. These arrived in January 1914 and the first successful hatching of a king penguin chick took place in 1919. The first penguins ever to be seen anywhere outside of their homeland, their fame quickly spread and the zoo has been in the forefront of the care and science of penguins ever since.

Left King penguin, iconic species

One of the most popular visitor attractions over the years is the daily penguin parade. This began quite by accident when, in 1951, a keeper left a gate open by mistake. Nowadays the gate is opened deliberately at a set time every day throughout the summer, and the bolder members of the breed will often be found waiting for the grand opening and their chance to walk amongst the visitors. No animal has to take part, so there are some who are quite happy to be left in the comfort of their own territory in the shadow of the old house.

The centre of the original private estate, the Mansion House has, over the years, provided living accommodation for keepers, offices for administrators and a meeting place for visitors. It was originally a family home, begun in 1793 by the Keith family and extensively remodelled in the 1890s by the Macmillan family whose fortunes were based on the Melrose tea company. Now the house is even a place for weddings and in 1997 the great-great-granddaughter of one of the original Macmillan owners of the house was married there.

For some years the Mansion House has provided a bar and restaurant for use by the members and their guests. The food is good and plentiful. The same could not be said for the zoo animals during the two world wars that were waged during the twentieth century. The outbreak of a major war so soon after the setting up of the zoo created major problems for all concerned. Keepers went off to fight and in 1918 the director found himself with only three men and two girls to feed, clean and generally look after the whole of the animal collection. With such horror happening overseas, it is interesting to note that visitor numbers remained quite high during the four years of the war. Doubtless the distraction of a day in beautiful surroundings with animals that were not fighting each other was part of the appeal.

Like keepers, but even more critically, food became increasingly scarce as the war went on. The cost of providing hay and grain rose considerably. For a while, the brown bears, for example, could be fed nothing but potato peelings from the restaurant. An appeal was put out to the fellows of the Society (who would these days be known as members) for extra funds to plug the gap between income and expenditure. Thankfully they responded generously and the zoo survived to go on to bigger and better things

Similar privations were experienced during World War II. The fighting came somewhat closer to home during this period and several bombs were dropped near or around the zoo. The only casualties reported were a few budgerigars and a chimpanzee that died of shock. It was during the first winter of this war that, once again the fellows of the Society were invited to send in money – this time specifically to pay for a particular animal's food – and this laid the foundation of what is now called the Animal Adoption scheme, which generates more than £100,000 per year for the animals' upkeep.

One of the more appealing outcomes of the war was the presentation to the zoo in 1946 of a brown bear called Wojtek. This much loved character had been adopted when a young cub as the mascot of the 22nd Company of the Polish Army Service Corps (Artillery). Wojtek died in 1963.

Another greatly loved animal was a chimpanzee called Philip that was given to the zoo in 1933. In early life as a captive pet, he had developed a fondness for cigarettes and alcohol, particularly, it is reported, port. Philip died aged 29, in 1963, a reasonably good age for a chimpanzee and apparently none the worse for his predilections.

Such stories serve to illustrate something of the problem faced by zoos as, over the years, a

The ever-popular penguin parade continues to this day, but camel and elephant rides are distant memories

greater vigour was applied to the study of the animals and the understanding of their welfare needs. Always and unashamedly a public attraction, nevertheless the emphasis of the work has changed.

Where once camels and elephants provided rides for visitors now the safari experience is offered on the back of a motorised trailer. No longer is it seen to be acceptable to use the larger zoo animals in this way. And where once the chimpanzees' tea party was a regular attraction, the animals' more natural, everyday behaviour is now seen as equally entertaining, if not more so, and much more illuminating.

There has not been an elephant in Edinburgh Zoo since the last one left for Windsor Safari Park in 1989. Greater study of their nature and habits led to the view that this huge herd animal, with its complex social arrangements, needed far more structure in its management in captivity than could be provided at that time.

Zoo staff do not regret such changes in attitude as they see the constant need to ensure that only the best of care is given to their charges. Every modern zoo must take into account the best of research, some of which takes place within the collection itself.

The essentially wild nature of the animals means that, over the years, escapes have taken place. During the last century these include a wolf, a polar bear, a brown bear and two sea lions. This latter pair was found in the Water of Leith a mile away at Roseburn after a three-hour chase in 1924.

Telling people about such stories has always been important. Dealing with wild animals is never going to be all plain sailing and it is crucial that members of the general public can have a proper understanding of what the zoo aims to achieve in its work.

From its inception, with its stated aim 'to foster and develop among people an interest in and knowledge of animal life', education has been at the heart of the Society's activities. It has also worked hard, through the national Zoo Federation (now called the British and

Irish Association of Zoos and Aquariums) to ensure that this became enshrined in law, so that the provision of appropriate education programmes would be a requirement of all zoos around the country.

Not surprisingly, therefore, Edinburgh Zoo was the first in this country to set up a dedicated education department. In the early 1970s the appointment of an education officer was an important landmark. The service to young people was taken up very quickly and the rapid development of the department in providing relevant and stimulating educational programmes provided a benchmark for zoo education, not only in Britain, but around the world.

From the beginning, building on much useful earlier work, the education department was a pioneer. A programme called Interlink, based on teaching the unity of the natural world, was developed in collaboration with a number of other Edinburgh organisations, such as the Botanic Gardens and the National Museums, where many common and complementary themes could be explored.

A unique component of every class visit was a walkabout in the zoo park that was directed and interpreted by the education officer. These walkabouts were and still are one of the special features of the education programme in Edinburgh.

From very early on there was a focus on the needs of the school curriculum and the

education department has continued to run excellent in-service courses for teachers to enable them to best use the marvellous resource that is found in the zoo and its animals, both in its work at home and overseas.

Not only does this work include the RZSS conservation projects in other countries, but also the latest idea, called the Global Classroom, which links schools across Scotland with educational establishments on other continents. Using the latest satellite communications technology, Global Classroom is helping young people learn from each other about their different environments, and the shared need for a responsible approach to wildlife conservation.

It has always been thought important that visitors to the zoo meet with the reality of the natural world in every part of the globe.

Over the years there has been a growing awareness that some of our native species are not as common as they might be, because habitat loss does not just happen overseas. Consequently in 1986, the Society acquired an estate in Kincraig, near Kingussie in the Highlands of Scotland. Nestling below the Cairngorm mountains the Highland Wildlife Park is home to some fifty species of native animals, some of which are extinct in the wild in Scotland.

It had been opened in 1972 by the then owner of the spectacular estate, Sir Andrew Forbes Leith, to show off a rapidly disappearing range of native species for visitors. Since its acquisition by the Society in 1986 as a companion to the zoo, it has been developed to take visitors back to a time before man's invasion of Scotland in 6,000 BC when bison, wolves, lynx, wild boar and wild horses roamed free in the Highlands.

On a lighter historical note, the Park's very own red grouse was the star of a major advertising campaign for its 'famous whisky' namesake.

Perhaps this story of a bird filmed in its most natural setting tells about the way in which animals can continue to be presented for the delight of visitors without quite the exploitation of previous times.

Above The red deer herd at the Highland Wildlife Park

Zoo Questions

With around 200 species and 1,500 animals kept in the two zoo parks it is no surprise that there are large numbers of staff dedicated to their care. The keepers in the zoo come from a variety of backgrounds. Regardless of academic qualifications, all of them undergo rigorous training in animal welfare and management, and constantly strive to achieve best practice as they work.

Naturally there are as many different attitudes to the job as there are people. Some keepers take special pleasure in working with individual animals – particularly the larger mammals – and are happy to form as close a bond with them as possible. They will have familiar names for each one and are pleased to introduce them to the visitors. Others take a more detached view and work from a more global standpoint. They may seem more dispassionate, but that does not mean that they lack passion about the subject of animals and their welfare.

As in all spheres of life, the variety of perspectives makes for a more rounded view. This is useful when it comes to considering the many difficult questions facing those who care about the work of zoos.

First and foremost, of course, is the whole question of captive and wild animals. Why should humans want to keep animals away from their natural wild habitat? What right have we to put them on view for our interest and pleasure? Isn't that somewhat selfish?

Needless to say such questions need dealing with, but there is unlikely to be a simple answer. It is possible to argue that displaying well cared-for animals in good captive conditions can be used to benefit the whole of the animal world. The wonder of seeing living examples, content with their lot, will enable the telling of the story of others in the wild. Rare and threatened species can be preserved in humane conditions while the problems that have led to their endangerment can be worked on and dealt with. The value of education in the business of conservation cannot be stressed enough and zoos have a valuable contribution to make in this field.

Nature is an extraordinary thing and it is amazing how the natural world finds solutions to its problems. But it is also a delicate thing and too often the so-called civilised human world intrudes uncomfortably into the wild. Regrettably we often need to intervene to put right the problems caused by our carelessness, thoughtlessness or selfishness. In the twenty-first century we can do great things and that is

Previous page Japanese serow (IUCN status: Lower Risk/Conservation Dependent)

Right Sea lions learning to respond to different commands

the problem. Little that we do these days is on a small, sustainable scale.

If we chop down trees for our commercial use, then we do it on a grand scale. Thus within weeks, a whole tract of unique rainforest can be reduced to nothing but bare earth and lots of valuable logs. A single tree in a rainforest may contain as many as 10,000 animal residents. And at a stroke we can make them homeless.

In the wild, plants and animals form and live in communities that interact with each other and the non-living aspects of their environment such as air and water, soil and rock. Under particular climatic conditions they form an eco-system in which everything has its unique and important part to play. Scientists are constantly learning about these relationships and there is much concern about the ways in which we are

all helping to upset the natural balance of things because of our perceived needs.

Most people in the zoo community themselves believe that in an ideal world there would be no need for zoos. However, given the world is as it is, one of the strongest arguments in favour of zoos is the role that they play in helping the public understanding of the natural world and the need to protect it. Education and research have long been fundamental to the philosophy of good zoos around the world.

Even with this general principle agreed, there are many questions facing the zoo community which engender discussion and great debate, and many topics on which there are differing ideas.

Longevity is one such topic. There is no doubt that zoo animals remain alive much longer than they might in the wild. The protection from natural predators and the constant provision of a plentiful supply of nutritious food and veterinary support means that, in truth, many will survive beyond what might be regarded as a natural lifespan. Most animals that die in captivity undergo a *post mortem* examination and there is evidence (for example in fused bones) that sometimes in aging captive animals there might have been a degree of pain or discomfort that could have been avoided if they had died at their 'natural' age in the wild.

No one wants that, but the high profile of a much-loved individual animal means that it is not always easy to persuade people of the need for euthanasia. It is often a very difficult decision for keepers and vets to make, as it is with many of us when it comes to our domestic pets. At what point should an animal be 'put down'?

Overleaf View from the African Plains towards the Pentland Hills

Similar ethical issues need to be faced when considering the breeding of animals. If a pair of animals is regarded as having a high 'mean kinship value', where they are genetically important to the conservation programme and are well matched, then they are encouraged to produce young. The general aim is to maintain something like ninety-five to ninety-nine per cent of that species' genetic pool for the next 100 years. Computer models play a large part in this calculation and so the theory appears quite safe.

However, the practice of breeding in captivity does throw up some dilemmas.

An example might be to take two Amur (formerly called Siberian) tigers, regarded to have mean kinship value and able to fulfil the important task of adding to the gene pool of the world population of this critically endangered species. A zoo may successfully breed two litters of three cubs from this pair. This effectively secures the genes from these animals and so there will be no more recommendations to breed from these individuals. There are, after all, only a finite number of places where the offspring can be put: there is only so much enclosure space in

Amur tigers, whose survival depends on conservation programmes

the world and native habitats are unlikely to be suitable for a reintroduction. The female tiger will probably be given contraception to prevent further pregnancies, or she or the male could be neutered.

Had this pair been in the wild they would have continued to breed with regular litters being produced, but with a high mortality rate for the young animals. Thus 'recruitment' in the wild is much slower than in captivity. Might it be more natural, then, for zoos to maintain a 'breed and cull' policy?

Could it be that in order to get six healthy new tigers it would be better to breed from the female every two years and cull two of the cubs each time? Thus the mother would rear one baby every eighteen months and six tigers would come over a twelve to thirteen year period rather than the shorter three-year period. It can be argued that the female animal would go through her full biological cycle in this way – perhaps better for her and the surviving cubs?

This breed and cull policy is pursued with some success in Denmark. There, it seems, the experts and general public have been convinced that this is the right way to do things. In Edinburgh, and throughout most of Europe, however, that is not the case, but the debate does continue.

The zoo has an animal welfare committee, made up of experts in the field that regularly considers this and other such issues. Their task is not an easy one and members of the zoo staff are encouraged to read up on the subject and attend international conferences where current science is explored and understandings are discussed.

Another constant discussion that takes place is that about which species the zoo should choose to keep. With an estimated 30 million species of which 29 million are invertebrates (and one in four of these are beetles) it can be difficult to decide. The delicate balance of nature means that the loss of even the smallest insect can have an impact on the whole of the ecological chain.

Sometimes a decision can be made because of the particular expertise of one member of the staff. For example in Edinburgh, in a little shed behind the reptile house, a remarkable conservation story is being acted out. Thanks to the interest and expertise of one man backed by an enthusiastic team, no fewer than seven varieties of partula snail have been saved due to pioneering husbandry work. Extinct in the wild, these small and apparently insignificant creatures are now held in other zoo collections and are providing an important continuation for the wildlife of the French Polynesian island of Moorea.

Other, perhaps more spectacular, animals that have their place in Edinburgh's collection include some that are particularly revered in their country of origin. Mishmi takin and gorals from China, Bactrian wapiti from Kazakhstan and its neighbouring countries and serow from Japan are all to be found in the zoo.

Mishmi takin
(IUCN status: Vulnerable)

Goral (IUCN status: Vulnerable)

Not only can the zoo help in the conservation of these species, but also they provide much excitement for visitors from home and abroad.

Two of the twenty-five most endangered species, the broad-nosed gentle lemur and purple-faced langurs, are part of the collection, here for both the protection of the species and the interest and delight of the visitor.

It is possible for an animal species to be rare but not necessarily endangered. In this case, the keeping of such species, for example the ring-tailed lemurs, can provide for an attractive and interesting exhibit that will point to other similar group of animals for purposes of education.

So, there are many reasons why particular species of animal are kept. All have their place in the whole that will make up a full experience for the visitor, sending him or her away with a renewed interest in and concern for the natural world in all its glory.

Some of the animals might be kept in the zoo because a particular research project is taking place or because there is a special connection with an *in situ* conservation project in their country of origin. The interest of a scientist may be different from that of the general visitor, but the individual animal probably doesn't know or care!

The work of scientists is clearly important in attempting to build a body of knowledge that will help with the preservation of natural behaviour and sustainable use of habitats. Close observation of zoo animals can be of enormous benefit to scientists working in the field. It is interesting to note that when one of Edinburgh's penguin keepers spent time observing king penguins in their natural habitat in the Falkland Islands, she was able to tell other researchers why the animals they were observing were behaving in a particular way. She had seen and been able to interpret and make sense of the natural behaviour at close quarters in the zoo.

An understanding of the habitat where animals live can be vital in all sorts of ways. Zoo people are acutely aware that animals most usually become endangered because the natural balance of their lives and their habitat is upset in some way. This can be due to many things, for example over-hunting, grazing of domestic livestock, tourism, pollution or environmental damage. More usually it is a combination of one or more of these and other factors.

The problem for the world is clear. How can we continue to enjoy our world and improve the living conditions of our fellow beings while at the same time preserve our precious and delicate natural resources? We all have a part to play and zoos do their bit, too, by inspiring, teaching and guiding us.

Zoo babies, like this young ring-tailed lemur, are always great favourites

Few in the zoo world believe that there are easy answers and all want to help in any way that they can. By caring for a number of the world's animals, by sharing knowledge and careful species management, by working with other concerned agencies to protect, restore and build habitats, by engaging the general public in a positive way, zoos are doing all that they can to ensure the preservation of animals and their habitats.

Finally, the question of whether an endangered species, rescued by captive breeding and care, can be reintroduced back into the wild is a tricky one. Some animals have been successfully put back to repopulate an area where the habitat has been secured in a suitable way, but such reintroductions are by no means easy. Animals become endangered often because their habitat has been compromised in some way and it is necessary to get together a number of agencies to work with local governmental systems and communities to deal with the many complexities that arise.

Edinburgh Zoo has been involved in the successful reintroduction back into the wild of scimitar-horned oryx and addax. Many valuable lessons about the planning, the necessary veterinary support and the need for constant monitoring have been learned and other species are sure to benefit in the future.

It will be seen that besides being a place of recreation for the visitor – where we can enjoy seeing healthy, active animals up close – a zoo also is offering a place for the proper care of a group of animals, for extensive and vital education, for research to better understand particular species and as a base for conservation work. All of these aspects of the work need to be reconciled. It is not easy, but it is possible and Edinburgh Zoo brings together these activities in a positive and enlightened way.

Addax, part of a reintroduction programme (IUCN status: Critically Endangered)

DAY AND NIGHT

'Can I speak to Jim Pansee, please?' It's a daft call, but not an uncommon one as yet another person is fooled by a friend into unwittingly ringing the zoo's number.

There's a lot that goes on behind the scenes in a zoo and it is not all about animals. The front line team on the reception desk are well used to calls for Miss C Lion and the like and they take it all in good part, along with the hundreds of other enquiries about opening times, looking after an exotic pet or advice on the weather conditions in Edinburgh.

A cheerful telephone manner is one of the requirements for the job of receptionist, but that certainly is not the only one. Selling tickets, encouraging gift aid donations (the proceeds of which are worth a great deal of money towards the work of the Royal Zoological Society of Scotland), answering general queries as to the whereabouts of the nearest lavatory or a particular animal, or helping to find the parents of a lost child are all part of a day's work for the reception staff.

The zoo is open to visitors every day of the year – including Christmas day. On the busiest day of the year more than 7,000 visitors come in through the gates. The quietest day may have as few as twenty-five. Christmas day can see around 400 people visiting to share the day with the animals and, perhaps, to avoid some of the general human excesses of the season.

With more than 600,000 visitors coming through the gates each year, there are a lot of extra things to do with people that need dealing with. The keepers ensure the welfare and contentment of the animals; others are dedicated to the welfare and happiness of the visitors.

Second only as a paying visitor attraction to Edinburgh Castle in Scotland, the zoo must constantly renew its appeal to the general public. Nearly 20,000 people are 'members' which effectively gives them a season ticket and an extra stake in the work of the Society. Their sense of ownership must be encouraged and the more casual visitor should leave with a feeling that they have been given a valuable and worthwhile experience.

The marketing department is always looking for topical and relevant ways to attract more visitors and tell the zoo's news. This might be through working with other agencies such as VisitScotland or the local bus companies with a money off offer on the back of their tickets. Regular advertising campaigns also use the sides of buses, public hoardings and television or newspaper advertising. Most days the press and public relations section will deal with media enquiries or send out information, the results of which will be read in the newspapers or seen on television. All of this activity will help bring people through the gate.

It is then that the hard work of others kicks in.

The car park attendant will make sure that the car is safely parked before the visitor is directed to the entrance to be sold a ticket. With the ticket comes a map, which is updated regularly by the zoo's in-house graphic designers.

Then it is probably time for a trip to the loo. Somebody is keeping them clean. Should the visitor want a cup of tea or an ice cream, then that is the responsibility of the catering staff, who run a number of top-rate food outlets and restaurants around the zoo. More than 120,000 portions of ice cream are sold annually in the park and this is the highest number in any visitor attraction in Scotland.

So, then it is out into the park. A 'hilltop safari' trailer is ready to take parties to the top of the hill and on the way they will be offered an informative commentary. Throughout the park there are volunteer helpers ready to give

---

Previous page Hand-reared king penguin chick

Right A warm welcome for every visitor

directions and to pass on fascinating facts and figures and something of their own passion for the animals. This small band of people comes from all walks of life and during the main summer season they give generously of their time for the love of the zoo and the animals.

The education staff of the zoo work daily with school and youth groups, helping them to understand more about the natural world, as well as working with general visitors through their engaging public talks and presentations. There is also someone whose job is 'interpretation' – ensuring that necessary information is offered to help visitors to understand more about the animals, their habitats and conservation issues. People come to see the animals, but they are also happy to learn if the information is presented in a way that is accessible and fun. Interpretation panels are put up alongside enclosures, but that may not be enough, so much thought goes into the different ways by which a story can be told. Events, animal encounters, trails and the guidebook all have a role here.

Another way might be through a book or an item on sale in one of the zoo's gift shops. The shop staff source and sell an exciting range of products that relate to the animal collection and this adds to the overall experience for visitors. It is always good to take a souvenir home or to send a postcard to friends or family. Even in the shops, the visitor can help make a difference. All the profits support the Zoo, of course, and with a wide variety of Fair Trade gifts for sale with some of the profits going to conservation projects in the wild, shoppers can help contribute to the good of people and animals on the other side of the globe.

The most popular animals sold in the gift shops are the cuddly penguins, with snakes being the most popular toy. Such facts are all recorded for future planning.

The administrative staff team is comparatively small, but they deal with all the activities behind the scenes that help to keep the zoo running efficiently. Bills and wages have to be paid, staff recruited and trained, computers repaired and the membership and animal adoption schemes operated. Most importantly, charitable funds have to be raised to provide for the vital conservation work that is carried out both at the zoo and in the wild. Yet more money must be found through the fundraising department to help develop the site and to provide for an even richer environment for the animals.

It is no surprise to learn that it is people that make the work of the zoo happen and great skills are harnessed from across all of the disciplines of those on the payroll and those who give of their time as volunteers.

Specific training takes place within the various sections or departments, to ensure that appropriate skills are developed, and more universal training is actively encouraged. Staff from all departments may be brought together for training in the use of computers or in customer service, for example, as these skills are vital to almost everyone working at the zoo. Every one of the zoo's staff is charged with being a good advocate for the zoo and the animals in its care. Nobody works in isolation and the friendly passing on of specialist knowledge by a keeper can help make a visit one of the best.

The natural world is not just represented by the animals in the collection. The hillside park that contains Edinburgh Zoo has two main purposes. It is a place where animals live and are cared for and it is a major visitor attraction. Because of this dual purpose there is a large team of men and women whose main job is to work with others to maintain and care for the grounds and buildings of the zoo.

A great deal of thought and work goes into this aspect of the place. Play areas and lawns, flowerbeds and trees all help to enhance the visitor experience. Within the park are many interesting and important plants and trees. In the eighteenth century, long before the zoo took over the park, some of the site was a nursery run by Thomas Blaikie who was responsible for planting many great French parks including the famous La Bagatelle near Paris

Two of the 120 or so species of tree are named after the apple cultivars John Downie and James Grieve, both gardeners who gave their name to the type of apples they developed here.

In 2003 a wildlife garden was developed by the gardening staff with help from volunteers and funded by a grant from Earthwatch. The garden demonstrates various ways to encourage wildlife into domestic gardens. Piles of logs, for example, will encourage small mammals and insects, and growing ivy will offer ideal nesting places for small birds and nectar for insects. Once again it can be seen that the Royal Zoological Society of Scotland is always trying to extend its reach and the interests of those with whom it comes into contact.

All of the public spaces are beautifully and sensitively planted with areas of grass, trees, shrubs and flowers. Alongside the fauna, there is recognition that the flora also have a part to play in the pleasure that can be given to a discerning public; be this through the shade of a tree in sun or rain, or the beauty of a bank of flowers offering a glorious springtime display.

But that is not all. Each of the animal enclosures contains a well-thought out selection of plants that are designed to enhance the lives of the animals. Some provide food or shelter, others offer a perch or nesting place; a dead branch might be the ideal hiding place for a small animal or even to reveal a bit of food that can be discovered by a busy forager.

Water plays an important part in many of the enclosures. A steam or a pond can greatly enhance the natural look of the space and it can also provide lots of opportunities for the animals to drink, wash or play. Much of this water is kept clean by a clever use of natural reed beds which filter the water in an environmentally-friendly way, thus reducing the need for mechanical and chemical systems.

Left Splashes of colour enhance the visitor experience

Right The duck ponds offer a haven of tranquility

The ground staff have an all-year round job but it tends to be busiest in the growing summer season when visitor numbers are at their highest. Grass is cut, paths are swept, flower beds dug and replanted; it is a never-ending task.

Teamwork is a key word in the zoo, and perhaps this is best seen in the building and maintaining of the animal enclosures. Ground staff will work with keepers to ensure that the best possible balance of planting is achieved. They will also work with the estate staff in the provision of nesting boxes for the birds or of swinging ropes or sleeping spaces for the mammals.

Each worker has something to contribute to the whole that makes for a good place to live and a good place to visit.

Visitors may pass one of the gardeners caring for the grounds or a crew of the estate staff building or maintaining an enclosure. If they are in army uniform then that might be one of the service groups that help with building by giving muscle power while learning teamwork and useful extra skills – the climbing frames in the chimpanzee enclosure and lots of the bongo enclosure owe much to their assistance.

Those with their own pets will not be surprised to hear of the importance of the veterinary team to the zoo.

Chimpanzee frame being built by the University of Aberdeen's Officer Training Corps

Gardening team clearing snow from paths around the park

Edinburgh Zoo is fortunate to work closely with the Royal (Dick) School of Veterinary Studies at the University of Edinburgh. Thanks to this partnership, the zoo has the largest specialist veterinary team in Exotic Animal Medicine in the UK. With five vets available, there are at least two clinical visits to the zoo every week for routine surgeries and the team is always on call for emergencies.

With so many different animals of all sizes and temperaments, the vets face many challenges. They work closely with the keepers, who naturally know their animals extremely well; and if there is a specialist job to do it is always good to have extra pairs of hands available. Also, of course, a familiar keeper can often help calm an animal in potentially stressful circumstances.

A great range of specialist and very expensive medical equipment is available for the performance of procedures and operations that range from helping with birth through soothing bite wounds, vaccinations and dental treatment to repairing fractured bones and removing tumours. For example, the zoo owns

Above Lioness receiving root canal treatment

Below Gorilla having tooth extracted

a range of specialist scales that allows the vets and keepers to weigh animals as tiny as a newly hatched chick weighing only a few grammes, right up to a fully adult male rhino, weighing up to three tons. Accurate weights are essential for calculating the correct drug dosages for a sick animal.

Diagnosing the problem is not always easy and there is an X-ray machine to help. Anaesthetics are administered, breathing is monitored and the patient is kept alive with other support equipment, much of which is not unlike that used in hospitals for humans – and it is certainly just as expensive.

As might be expected, much of the work carried out will give increased knowledge that can be passed on to others in the form of written reports and the presentation of scientific papers. In addition, the veterinary team is involved with much interesting and useful ongoing research. This increases the general knowledge base for Edinburgh's animals, as well as those in other zoos and their counterparts in the wild.

It can even help the human race. The Phantasmal poison arrow frog (*Epipedobates tricolour*), for example, has been found to have a chemical that is about 200 times more potent than morphine, in laboratory tests. Researchers in America are hoping to mimic its effects to develop medicines to block pain.

Others who come in from outside to work occasionally in the zoo park are the registrars who preside over marriages. The Society holds a civil licence for the holding of marriage ceremonies and these are not confined to the Mansion House. One couple was married with the polar bear as a witness as it was just in front of her enclosure that the man proposed and had his offer accepted.

Other great life events have in the past been marked with the scattering of ashes in a place loved by the recently departed.

More common are special events such as conferences and parties at what must be one of the most unusual venues in Edinburgh. Out of hours special tours are offered which give a privileged look at the animals as they prepare for the night or rise early in the morning. The zoo is a great place for children's parties and the youngsters are offered a mini-tour, games and a tea party. Many adults are happy to enjoy a similar experience.

Those who book the Mansion House in the centre of the park might be warned to watch out for ghosts, as reports of spectres haunting the old house have been made at regular intervals. It is said that a grey lady walks the corridors and a rather distinguished gentleman can be seen in the window of the coffee lounge first thing in the morning…

He may be one of the first to see the early morning work of the keepers and garden staff.

Overnight there are regular security patrols and keepers living in the park are on call for any emergencies. Most of the animals settle down to rest or sleep during the hours of darkness, but there is always someone on hand if there is a sick animal or an expectant mother that needs monitoring.

Left Phantasmal frog: a leap forward in medical research?

Right Preparing fruit for tropical birds

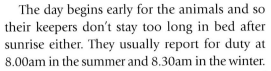

The day begins early for the animals and so their keepers don't stay too long in bed after sunrise either. They usually report for duty at 8.00am in the summer and 8.30am in the winter.

Every animal in the zoo has a team of dedicated people whose job it is to look after their welfare. There is much to do. Enclosures need to be kept clean and the environment constantly monitored so that the animals remain in the best condition.

Nothing is left to chance and those working with the animals take every opportunity for reading and finding out more about their particular species in order to understand what is most appropriate for them. They will know all there is to know about conditions in the wild and are in constant touch with other animal keepers throughout the world, sharing and exchanging information and ideas.

Better still, a constant close observation of the individuals in their care is the real source of knowledge. The keeper will know when an individual is a bit 'off colour' and may need some extra special care. Perhaps it will need a change to its diet or occasionally veterinary attention. Careful monitoring ensures that the welfare of each animal is properly looked after, and our keepers are actively involved in research that contributes to the ever-evolving science of animal care.

In all of the different animal care sections, the keepers begin their day with a visit to the enclosures for which they are responsible to ensure that all is well. Once satisfied, they get stuck into the relentless task of cleaning and making sure that there is nothing in the area that should not be there.

Unfortunately some of the visitors are not as sensible as they should be and will occasionally throw things into enclosures.

Left Collecting lime tree leaves as browse for the bongo

Sometimes a high wind will blow in rubbish. This can be very dangerous for the animals, so it is important to be vigilant. A small army of people go all around the zoo each evening and throughout the day to pick up litter and to empty all of the bins before the foxes or squirrels get at them.

As the zoo is open every day of the year, there will always be visitors to talk to and the keepers can proudly chat about their work and 'their' animals. But they must be forgiven if they rush off, for there is always work to do. The breeding season in the spring and summer is an especially busy time, with nests and nurseries to be checked. New penguin chicks, for example, are weighed every day and careful monitoring and records kept of their progress from hatching, through feeding and eventual independence from their parents.

And every day of the year, food has to be prepared. There is quite a science to this. It is vital that a correct balance of nourishment is offered. As far as possible, all of the animals are given food identical or very similar to that they would eat in the wild. Often this food is hidden around the enclosure so that searching for it becomes a stimulating activity, and helps to encourage natural behaviour.

The giant anteater (*Myrmecophaga tridactyla*), for example, can find some of its food in an old Wellington boot, so that it has to use its specially adapted long snout to search out the tasty morsels. The chimpanzees will use a stick to root about in a specially built rock in their enclosure, simulating a termite mound, to extract delicious treats like apple juice or honey. The keepers are constantly finding ingenious ways of offering the food in a way which is more stimulating for the animals and, by happy co-incidence, is also more interesting for the visitors.

Provision of food is a major activity, and the stores figures are astonishing. More than 41 tons of mackerel, herring, blue whiting and sprats, costing £21,000, feed the fish-eaters while 18 tons of meat from horses, calves, deer and pigs, costing £11,000, is bought in for the carnivores. Rabbits, rats, mice, chicks and quails (some 165,000 individuals costing £34,000) add variety and food for the smaller meat eaters. The herbivores eat their way through hundreds of bales of horse haige and lucerne costing more than £13,000. In addition to this, tons of pellets, costing £20,500, and supplements and vitamins, costing £10,000, are added to the mix.

Some of the necessary food is grown within the zoo park and £11,000 worth of insects is bought in for breeding and feeding purposes. Fruit and vegetables are donated by supermarket groups Sainsbury and Marks & Spencer and by the banana importers Fyffes. Such giving is, of course, a great help where budgets are concerned.

This is not the only contact that the zoo has

with supermarkets. It is not uncommon for a telephone call to be received asking for help in identifying and caring for exotic animals found in imported boxes. Incidences of insects and scorpions – not a speciality of the zoo – are referred to the Butterfly and Insect World in Lasswade, but all others, such as frogs, snakes and snails, come in to the zoo or are referred to the SSPCA.

The penguins are given dead fish to eat. It is against legislation to feed live vertebrates to the animals (although insects can be fed to amphibians in the reptile house), so buckets of herring, whiting and sprats are prepared with supplements of vitamins and minerals to compensate. These are fed whole, by hand four times a day to the birds. Other species receive their food in many different feeding regimes and methods, according to their need and as far as possible replicating their life in the wild.

Also via the stores section, bedding is provided with on average 28 tons of straw and 600 bales of shavings being delivered annually.

With such costs the animal adoption scheme is a great help in paying for the care of individual animals. Introduced during the second world war, members of the public can help support the huge costs of feeding the animals, heating their houses, enriching their enclosures and providing excellent veterinary treatment. Adopting an animal at Edinburgh Zoo or the Highland Wildlife Park can help to make a real difference to the individual animals, but can also be a lovely way to mark a birthday or anniversary or even just to show a special interest in a favourite animal.

There are so many incidental costs, for example a keeper's uniform costs £200 per year, so all help beyond the usual public entry

Right Straw for animal bedding being moved to storage in the barn

fees and money earned from the commercial activities is gratefully received.

Sometimes extra money is earned from the fees associated with filming and the zoo has provided locations for episodes of the television series 'Taggart' and 'Rebus' and for various programmes such as Blue Peter and Rolf Harris' Animal Hospital, although fees are waived if the items promote the welfare and conservation work of the zoo.

Advertising agencies occasionally come up with zany ideas for commercials featuring animals and just so long as there is no stress on the animals then photographs or filming might be allowed. The star of the Famous Grouse whisky advertisements was photographed at the Highland Wildlife Park, but only after days of extremely careful preparation so that the bird was completely relaxed. A health education 'healthy walking' campaign featured a well-known Scottish

rugby player stepping out in front of the penguins as they, blithely unaware, took part in their daily parade.

Like all of the animals when content, the penguins get on with their lives doing what comes naturally. They seem not to mind being looked at by our visitors and, indeed, many of them choose to join in the daily voluntary 'penguin parade' when a group of them walk out of the enclosure and take a stroll around the lawn to the delight of those watching.

The fact that they might appear in a thousand photograph albums and in millions of the day's papers matters nothing to them.

Famous faces are often seen in the zoo quietly enjoying a day out with their families. At other times they will be seen in a more public light posing for cameras, perhaps as part of a particular fundraising event or campaign. Over the years, many Royal visitors have enjoyed being shown around, making a

welcome break to their more onerous official duties.

Sometimes those using the zoo for publicity purposes have very different agendas. Animal rights protestors occasionally come to Edinburgh to make a point. Zoo staff treat their views with respect and regular conversations do take place. The facts are presented and, if a common mind cannot be achieved, then there has to be an agreement to differ.

With concern for animal welfare enshrined in the work of the zoo, sometimes the pragmatic stance has to be taken that there may be two ways of looking at the same thing. Having to justify one's actions in the face of a criticism keeps everyone on their toes and, as long as the animals benefit from such exchanges of view, then all is well.

Happily, disagreements like this are rare and effective collaborations are much more common. A recent example of successful collaboration is the protection of a small species of mouse, unique and native to the islands of Canna and Sanday in the Inner Hebrides. Rats had been introduced from visiting ships and the growing population was threatening not only the important breeding site for several species of seabird, but also the native mice.

Consequently, the owners of the islands, the National Trust for Scotland, appointed the New Zealand-based Wildlife Management International to eradicate the rats by laying traps. Such an operation obviously would also threaten the indigenous mice, so the Royal Zoological Society of Scotland was called in to help capture and establish a breeding colony of 120 mice, which they would look after while the cull was taking place. The idea is then to reintroduce the mice once the island is free of the rat intruders.

Money for this project came from the European Union and the traps were made by inmates of Edinburgh's Saughton Prison. The

mice are currently being cared for and thriving both in the zoo and at the Highland Wildlife Park. Thus, through a highly collaborative effort, a native species will be preserved and soon will continue to thrive in its natural habitat. Conservation takes many forms, but it usually involves collaboration.

Another collaboration ensures the cleanliness of the penguin pool. Several local diving clubs regularly come, fully equipped to clean all of the glass in the viewing area of the pool and to vacuum some of the algae from the bottom of the pool. Such useful work is done with a spirit of great generosity and all have the satisfaction of seeing a job well done. Initially nervous of these strange creatures with hoses and flippers, the penguins soon came to trust the divers, and now swim alongside them with obvious enjoyment.

Needless to say, not everything in the zoo runs smoothly. The terrible Foot and Mouth disease crisis in 2001 meant that the place had to close for some weeks at the height of the outbreak, in order to protect the animals from potential disease. All those entering and leaving the zoo park were screened and disinfected in order to prevent any spread to the animals. Keepers and other essential staff had to shower and change their clothes in icy conditions, and even when the zoo re-opened, the bio-security measures remained in place for several months – even bridal parties had to step in disinfectant before being allowed up to the Mansion House!

Contingency plans are in place for a range of natural and man-made emergencies. The more recent threat of the spread of avian flu has led to the setting up of a small sub-committee of experts to advise on procedures if the deadly disease came into the country. Advice is available from government agencies and the national zoo body, BIAZA, so that an agreed protocol is properly in place before any problems arise.

Another very important bit of emergency planning is the zoo's escaped animal procedure, which takes place around four times a year. Actual escapes are very rare, but things must be in place just in case, and all staff have their part to play in ensuring that all goes smoothly. Some will be shepherding members of the public into buildings for their own safety, others will be closing gates and clearing the telephone system. One senior member of the animal department then co-ordinates an extremely rigorous procedure to track and, if necessary, sedate the animal. In the practice runs, the part of the animal is played by one of the keepers, and he or she may choose to hide in bushes for as long as it takes to be found!

The health and safety officer and several members of the animal department are fully trained in firearms, and receive regular refresher courses and testing in the use of guns with both tranquilisers and live ammunition in order to retain their licences.

The same health and safety officer (who describes his job as keeping the chief executive out of prison!) is responsible for an awesome range of activities from fire drills to first aid training. He works in what might be described as a small town, with everything from a blacksmith, a general stores and a butcher's shop to a hospital, restaurants and a village green. There are some 82 acres with nearly 100 buildings, from a kennel to the Mansion House. He must constantly remind staff that in the zoo unusual and sometimes dangerous things happen.

Very robust risk assessments of all the zoo's activities take place on a regular basis, and lessons are learned from 'near misses'. A human cold or a pregnancy might affect the animal population and *vice versa*, people can slip and fall on the sometimes steep hillside site, animals coming into the park need to be quarantined, wild bats in the area can cause problems, and so on, yet interestingly the most common injury is a wasp sting.

Lots of the staff, across all departments, are trained in first aid and help can quickly be on hand to solve any emerging problem or to call an ambulance if necessary.

Weather, of course, can become something of a problem – especially when you are trying to decide how many ice creams to order. Use of a very sophisticated five day weather forecast can help with the potential problem of the over or under ordering of cooling ices and can also help predict the days when, due to adverse conditions, the zoo will be quiet. With fewer visitors, plans can be made for getting much needed jobs done when staff are not needed to serve the visitors.

Right Blacksmith at work, one of the zoo's team of specialised craftsmen

Whatever the task, everyone at the zoo works extremely hard, and by way of relaxing and getting to know one another, they also play hard when given the opportunity. Throughout the year, there are many events organised, through the staff social committee, ranging from quiz nights, to bowling and barbecues. Staff – including the chief executive – have even been known to participate in fiercely competitive tug o'wars inside the rhino enclosure (with the rhinos safely in their indoor quarters of course) to raise money for a national children's charity. All these events serve to keep the staff in touch with colleagues in different departments, and also help them feel part of the whole.

Such is the complexity of the operation of Edinburgh Zoo and, by extension, the

THE ROYAL ZOOLOGICAL SOCIETY OF SCOTLAND

Highland Wildlife Park, that it is vital that all the constituent parts can work together well.

The badge of the Royal Zoological Society of Scotland shows a gannet soaring over the head of a zebra and a red heraldic lion. A penguin and a grey seal standing on rocks above the rolling waves of the sea support the shield. The motto that flows on the scroll over it says in Latin *Multiformis Sapientia Dei* which means 'the manifold wisdom of God' and hints at the wonders of creation. It even anticipates the importance of biodiversity which perhaps wasn't clearly understood at the time the motto was adopted.

The logo of Edinburgh Zoo itself is a king penguin in full underwater flight. For the Highland Wildlife Park, three animals leap in sequence as if in an ancient rock painting: Przewalski's horse, a bison and a stag.

So much is said in pictorial and heraldic form. It is all about the animals and nature. Perhaps the role of the human animal, in its many forms, which lives under these banners needs also to be celebrated.

MEAT EATERS ALL

We all have animals that are special to us and there are many reasons for choosing a favourite. Sometimes it is because we had a particular toy when we were young, sometimes it is because of an animal character in a children's book or cartoon film. We may have been particularly taken by one of the brilliant wildlife films that regularly appear on our screens.

Whatever the reason, many visitors will make a bee line for a particular enclosure in the zoo. Sometimes we are disappointed. The zoo does not look after every species. Scientists have identified more than one and a half million different kinds of plant and animal and more are being added to the list every year. It is thought that there could be as many as 30 million animal species in existence, so the task of identifying them all may never be complete.

All plants and animals, also known as flora and fauna, are classified by scientists according to a system that is based on an overall similarity between organisms. An eighteenth century Swedish botanist and explorer called Carolus or Carl Linnaeus introduced the classification system identifying all organisms by a two-part scientific name. The first part is the genus to which the animal belongs and the second its species. With each plant and animal having a generic and a specific label this enables every individual type of plant and animal to be identified throughout the scientific world in an agreed international language, Latin.

These scientific names are important. They avoid confusion and mean that scientists and all of those working with animals can be very clear with their individual identifications which act as signposts showing exactly how they fit into the natural world.

Fortunately, most animals in the zoo also go by a common name that is much easier for all concerned.

Edinburgh Zoo looks after a great variety of animals and it seems – from the toys sold in the gift shops and the animal adoptions, for instance – that the big cats are the visitors' favourite of all the animal groups.

In the hierarchical system of classification, these come from the kingdom or overall division *Animalia*, the phylum subdivision *Chordata*, which is further subdivided into the class *Mammalia* (and here we begin to be on familiar ground as this leads to our common word mammals), and then into the order *Carnivora* (carnivores), then to the family *Felidae* (all cats) and the genus *panthera* or *felis* and species names, for example, *tigris* – tiger or *sylvestris* – wild cat.

Felidae, or cats, eat little besides meat and as such are the most carnivorous of the carnivores. Superb predators, they are often at the top of the food chain. Found in habitats ranging from deserts to Arctic regions, there is a conservation crisis for the entire Felidae family. Hunting for their skins, use of body parts in traditional medicines and habitat destruction have all contributed to declining numbers in the wild.

There are more than 35 species in the cat family. Most have a strong muscular body, sharp claws and teeth, keen senses and quick reflexes.

Those known as the Big Cats have the ability to roar rather than purr…the lion, tiger, leopard, snow leopard and jaguar.

Their popularity in the zoo perhaps has something to do with our love for our own domestic cats (*Felis catus*). The animal population in the park does change from time to time, but favourites are usually to be found. All are fascinating to observe and every individual has his or her own look and ways of behaving. Naturally, though, each species has much in common.

Previous page Amur tiger
(IUCN status: Critically Endangered)

Right Asiatic lion (IUCN status: Critically Endangered)

Apart from the cheetah with its long muscular legs designed for the chase, cats tend to stalk and pounce upon their prey. Binocular vision enables them to judge distances so that this is an efficient and successful activity. Live prey is not too keen on becoming dead food, so the success of the hunt cannot be guaranteed; patience and persistence is required on the part of the hunter.

The zoo's cats are regularly fed on joints of fresh muscle meat but, in the wild, animals will go without food for three or four days (during which time they can sleep for up to 22 hours per day). Consequently in the zoo, the animals are given 'starve' days in order to replicate their wild conditions.

The beauty of big cat coats mean that they have often been hunted to near extinction in order that humans can enjoy the skin as a trophy or to wear. Fortunately, attitudes towards such hunting and killing have changed and now the fur can be properly admired where it best belongs: still being worn by a live animal! Close to, visitors to the zoo can see just how wonderful are the markings. At a bit of a distance and in their enclosures designed to reproduce wild habitat conditions it may be quite a different experience. Such is the brilliance of the camouflage, it is sometimes quite difficult to see the animal.

Animals in the zoo collection come from all parts of the world and the big cats are no exception.

The zoo has two female lions (*Panthera leo persicus*), sisters Gita and Kamlesh which were born in Chester Zoo in 1997. The male lion, Royal, was born in Helsinki in 2000. Unlike the African lion, the Asiatic lions are highly endangered in the wild, where there may be fewer than 300 remaining in India, in protected reserves in the Gir Forest. These three are part of an important European breeding programme.

In the wild, the roar can be heard up to five miles away. A roar can be used to warn off others and to reunite the male's scattered family. The zoo's neighbours have become quite used to these exotic sounds as they go about their everyday business.

Unlike tigers that seem to love it, lions are wary of water and will try to avoid having to swim in it. In very dry conditions, they get fluid to survive from the blood of their prey. Water is, of course, provided in the lion enclosure for drinking purposes.

The lions will be seen to be all in an enclosure together as they are the only truly social animals amongst the big cats. Males and females live in large family groups with their

Amur tiger (IUCN status: Critically Endangered)

offspring. They are also unique amongst the cat family in having distinct visible differences between the males and females. The male dominates prides, but it is the female that does most of the hunting and rearing of the young.

Tigers have a reputation and it seems that the zoo's young visitors are especially keen to meet them. In Edinburgh they will see a pair of Amur tigers (*Panthera tigris altaica*).

The female, Sasha, was born in Moscow Zoo in 1996, the offspring of wild parents which had been confiscated from poachers. The male, Yuri, was born in Duisburg, Germany in 1993. They have successfully reared two litters of triplets here at Edinburgh Zoo (in 2000 and 2003) and for the moment their breeding is suspended, as their genetic material is well represented within the conservation breeding programme.

Tigers are capable of dragging heavy prey that would take a group of six or more humans to move. Such power is exciting to witness and it can be a real treat to watch the animals feeding. Tigers have a rough tongue that is designed to peel skin off its prey and to rasp flesh off the bone.

Like so many species, they are territorial and will be seen patrolling and marking their space, even in the zoo. Amur tigers, the largest subspecies and the lightest in colour, have long, thick coats to keep them warm in the cold climate where they roam, in the far east of Russia, along the Amur river valley.

It is interesting to note that tigers do make a purring sound, but they purr only on the out breath. Domestic cats purr on both the in and out breath.

The jaguar (*Panthera onca*) is the New World's only big cat and it resembles a leopard. It prefers to be near water and is found in the wild near permanent swamps and forests that flood on a regular seasonal cycle. Although legally protected, this species is at risk because of the increasing destruction of its habitat and because cattle ranchers see it as a threat to their livestock.

The jaguar is happiest near water, but some carnivorous mammals have adapted to life in the water. They spend varying amounts of time in or out of the water depending on their biological and behavioural needs.

Below Jaguar (IUCN status: Near Threatened)

Sea lions spend almost all year in the water, coming onto land only for resting, breeding and giving birth. Over time, seals and sea lions have adapted perfectly to life at sea. Their legs have evolved into flippers and they have streamlined bodies that are well insulated with blubber against the cold water.

Like all Californian sea lions (*Zalophus californianus*) Edinburgh's three, Cowrie, Laura and Pebbles, are highly intelligent animals. The species rarely goes out more than 10 miles from land and often they can be found in estuaries and harbours where there is lots of food and shelter. The human activity in these places seems to stimulate the sea lions and so the keepers have devised a training regime for them. This keeps the animals stimulated and provides for their fish feeding activities.

They have learned to respond to simple commands for feeding and such a response can be very helpful when they need veterinary attention. Their lack of fear of humans enables the vet to get close enough without having to administer any tranquilising drugs. This is just as well, as on dry land the sea lion can still outpace a human!

Californian sea lion (IUCN status: Lower Risk)

Unlike sea lions, which move very clumsily on land, otters and polar bears are equally graceful on land and in the sea.

The award-winning enclosure for the otters at Edinburgh Zoo enables them to play in pools and down a fall of running water much to the delight of the visitor, as well as the otters themselves! These Asian small-clawed otters (*Aonyx cinerea*) are the smallest species of otter in the world. They live in freshwater wetlands and mangrove swamps throughout south Asia.

The female, Nipper, and her partner, Dennis, have successfully reared several litters of otter pups since moving into this spacious enclosure in June 2002. Solar panels on the roof of the east viewing hut provide heat for one of the lower pools and this is just one example of the zoo's desire to be as environmentally friendly as possible.

Much thought is going into the question of how the zoo can best house its polar bear (*Ursus maritimus*).

Left Asian small-clawed otter
(IUCN status: Near Threatened)

Right Polar bear
(IUCN status: Conservation Dependent)

Mercedes was rescued from the wild in 1983 to avoid being shot for being a 'nuisance' to the inhabitants of Churchill, Manitoba. She was named after the car manufacturer that sponsored her airlift from Canada, but her keepers still call her 39, the identification number that was painted in large red numbers on her side by the authorities in Manitoba. Since coming to Edinburgh she has successfully raised two cubs and proved a very attentive mother.

The damaging effects of climate change on the Arctic environment have caused polar bears to become conservation dependent, so the zoo's executive is discussing plans to build an enormous new underwater home for these wonderful creatures as part of the development master plan for the next few years.

Hot dry conditions somewhat without water are the more natural habitat of another of the zoo's popular carnivores, the meerkat (*Suricata suricatta*). Despite this, they thrive in Scotland's wet conditions, breeding regularly and adding to their numbers.

From very hot, sandy desert areas of southern Africa, these active members of the mongoose family live in large communal groups. The dominant female is the only one to breed, but they share all the tasks such as looking after the young, hunting for food and keeping a lookout for predators, particularly birds of prey.

Meerkat (IUCN status: Lower Risk)

While most of the members of the group forage or sun themselves (a very popular activity with this species) there will be at least one animal on a high point acting as sentry and lookout. In the zoo, visitors can hear them calling to each other and racing underground if they spot a seagull or helicopter flying overhead!

The keepers in Edinburgh Zoo name each new litter of meerkat babies with Biblical names, beginning with the next consecutive letter of the alphabet. The litter born in July 2004 are called Esther, Elijah, Esau, Ezra, Eve and Eli, and the next litter have names beginning with F, and so on.

Meerkats feed on various insects as well as scorpions, small lizards and even snakes. By contrast, the red panda (*Ailurus fulgens*) feeds on bamboo leaves and shoots. In addition it eats other vegetation along with grubs, small vertebrates such as lizards or mice, and birds' eggs and chicks.

Found throughout south Asia, on high forest slopes, these beautiful bear-like animals are distantly related to, but very different from, the giant panda. The main thing that they have in common is their love of bamboo and, regrettably, their increasingly rare status.

Somewhat solitary, red, or lesser, pandas are agile climbers which spend most of the daylight hours asleep, curled up in the tops of trees. They come down to look for food at dusk and dawn, so daytime visitors to the zoo need to look up.

Edinburgh Zoo is the only place in the UK that you will find one of the most elusive and unusual carnivores. The wolverine (*Gulo gulo*) lives in the forest and open tundra of northern America and across Eurasia. It looks rather like a bear but behaves more like a weasel. It is incredibly strong, an agile climber and

excellent swimmer, and it will even tackle prey as large as a caribou.

The zoo's females came to Edinburgh from Norden's Ark in Finland and Berne Zoo in Switzerland as part of the generous exchange of animals that takes place on a regular basis. The introduction of a male of the species will enable them to be bred as part of the worldwide captive breeding conservation programme.

It will be noted that all of the carnivores mentioned so far come from different continents and they might be regarded as a representative sample of the many smaller carnivore species in Edinburgh Zoo.

Right Red panda (IUCN status: Endangered)

Overleaf Snow leopard (IUCN status: Endangered)

The food for all of these meat eaters has to be bought in and prepared individually to be fed at the right time and in the most natural and interesting way to each of the species. A lot of the keepers' time is spent preparing a varied diet for the animals. Every diet is matched as carefully and accurately as possible to the animals' natural intake of food in the wild. Sometimes this means that supplements of vitamins and minerals are added to get just the right balance.

There is a stores department within the zoo and through it keepers can order what their animals need and want. More than 40 tons of fish are fed to the animals each year. Delicacies include nearly 7,000 rats, 60,000 mice, 90,000 chicks, 7,000 quail, 5,000 rabbits and nearly 19 tons of flesh from horses, calves, deer and pigs.

Some of these tasty meat joints are especially enjoyed by the wolves and painted hunting dogs. These carnivorous feeders offer an often dramatic scene for the visitor as they tear the meat apart in their hurry to feed.

It seems that all the wolves, foxes and dogs in the world are descended from the same common ancestor as our pet dogs at home. They all belong to the canid family, and share several common characteristics. In addition to being carnivores, they have very keen senses for smelling, hearing and seeing their prey. They also have specially adapted teeth, canines that are ideal for gripping and killing their prey, incisors for tearing into flesh and molars for crushing the bones.

Edinburgh's pack of painted hunting dogs (*Lycaon pictus*) – or African wild dogs as they are sometimes known – are an example of the most efficient carnivores in Africa, usually killing around 85 per cent of their intended prey. They can finish off a zebra in 20 minutes! Living and hunting in large, co-operative packs, they are extremely caring of their young

Painted hunting dog (IUCN status: Endangered)

and have strong social bonds. The zoo's group of five females came from Berlin Zoo where they had been named K1 – K5, but keepers have since named them Eve, Pip, Spot, Spice and Ginger. With the introduction of a pair of male dogs, the zoo will embark on a conservation breeding programme for this fascinating animal.

A senior figure from the Wild Conservation Research Unit of Oxford University spent much time imparting his knowledge of this species to the team of keepers. He sees an important role for zoos in the conservation work that he and his colleagues do, particularly in the research and observation. Veterinary research on drugs and vaccines done in zoos has been invaluable to *in situ* conservation programmes.

From a different continent, this time out of Central and South America, comes the bush dog (*Speothos venaticus*). Living mainly in Panama, Peru, Brazil and Parguay these small, stocky dogs were once numerous. Now they are being threatened by habitat loss as forests are cleared for settlement and logging.

They live sociably, in packs of around 10 animals, hunting together for small prey, particularly rodents. At night, they sleep in burrows or hollow tree trunks. The zoo with one male, Naos, and a female, Bella, as with so many species, is participating in the conservation breeding programme for this vulnerable animal.

Another from the canid family in the zoo's collection comes from the same continent. The maned wolf (*Chrysocyon brachyurus*) is a shy, elusive animal known in its native South America as the 'fox on stilts'. This is thanks to its extremely long legs that help it to move cautiously through the long grass in search of its prey of small rodents, birds, reptiles and insects. They also eat fruit.

In many ways the maned wolf is similar to Britain's own native red fox, which has much shorter legs, as it does not need to move through such long grass. Those long legs are an excellent example of the way in which nature adapts itself for a purpose. The animal's extra height allows it to peer over the low-scrub vegetation for both prey and danger.

Edinburgh's male, Blade, was born in Chester Zoo and the female, Eva, was born in Krefeld Zoo in Germany. Since their arrival at Edinburgh Zoo in 2000 they have successfully raised three litters of pups, as part of a European conservation breeding programme.

The captive breeding programmes carried out by all good zoos, in co-operation with each other and naturalists and scientists throughout the world, is of huge importance. If asked, most of the zoo staff would say that they prefer to see all animals in the wild, in their natural habitat. Unfortunately for a variety of reasons, not the least that that natural habitat may no longer exist, this is often not possible.

Consequently, zoos really do have an essential role to play in ensuring that endangered species continue to exist. At the same time as actively supporting conservation projects *in situ*, in the wild, zoo staff and supporters can ensure that a species is saved from extinction through carefully managed *ex situ* breeding programmes.

Very occasionally it is possible to re-introduce zoo-bred species back into the wild. In co-operation with other wildlife conservation organisations working to protect the remaining habitats and eco-systems, such animals can be protected until they are able to thrive again where they naturally belong. However, reintroduction of species to the wild is, of necessity, an extremely long-term and fragile process. Hence the need for zoos to retain 'back up' populations.

The keepers at Edinburgh Zoo keep meticulous records of all the animals born here, along with any subsequent illness, injury or death, and all this data is submitted to an international network of 'studbook keepers'. These studbooks form the basis for all the national, regional and international conservation breeding programmes, aiming to retain as much genetic diversity as possible. Through these studbooks, which are fully computerised, our keepers can talk to colleagues throughout the world and together they can bring together the best animals for breeding purposes, ensuring the most healthy and diverse gene pool possible.

Maned wolf (IUCN status: Near Threatened)

CLOSE COUSINS

Apes, monkeys and lemurs are all part of the group of mammals called primates, which also includes humans. In general, apes are larger than monkeys and lemurs, and have no tails. Much like the designation 'big cats' there is a category of primates popularly called the 'great apes'. These are the gorilla, chimpanzee, bonobo and orang utan, while the 'lesser apes' include all the gibbon species.

All apes share particular features that enable them to live successful lives in trees (though some species can spend most of their time on the ground). These include forward facing eyes that ensure the correct judging of distances and prehensile (grasping) hands and feet.

The lesser apes have arms that are generally longer than their legs, allowing them to swing through trees, which is called 'brachiation'. Monkeys and lemurs, on the other hand, tend to have longer legs than arms and they run along the tops of branches and leap from tree to tree.

In recent years scientists have carried out extensive studies of primate species, partly because of the need to find significant populations for purposes of conservation. Because of this research, there is a growing realisation that primates, with nearly 200 species, have exceptional diversity and many new species have been described in the past twenty or so years.

Edinburgh Zoo offers a good selection for the interest of visitors.

The largest of all the primates, sometimes known as Africa's gentle giants, gorillas (*Gorilla gorilla*) are herbivorous, eating only plant material. They are mild mannered and generally seek out ways of avoiding conflict if at all possible. They live in tight family groups, led by a protective male 'silverback' who decides where they sleep and look for food. Each night the gorilla will make itself a new nest.

Edinburgh's male is Sam Sam and his female partner is called Yinka, who came from Dublin Zoo. Both Western lowland gorillas were actually born in the wild, and were probably the last of the 'legal captures' from the wild. Nowadays, almost all the animals you see in zoos have been born in captivity.

Left and previous page
Gorilla (IUCN status: Endangered)

Found extensively throughout central Africa, chimpanzees (*Pan troglodytes*) are now listed as Endangered owing to the fragmentation of their habitat – rainforest and grassland – as well as the devastating effects of the bushmeat trade.

Generally recognised as the most intelligent primate after humans, you only have to watch the group for a few minutes to see the remarkable similarity to human society, with all its squabbling and affection in equal measure! They are obviously powerful and can be extremely aggressive animals. Such aggression is, of course, a product of the harsh environment in which the animals find themselves when in the wild and having to live off their wits and the strength and stability of their social group.

Chimpanzees are considered the closest living relative to human beings sharing 98.2 per cent of our genetic material. They communicate with each other using a wide range of facial expressions and calls, and they are one of the few animal species to use tools.

Such qualities make primates an obvious subject for research and the Royal Zoological Society of Scotland is working with the Scottish Primate Research Group to set up a unique primate study centre within the zoo park, housing squirrel and capuchin monkeys. The 'Living Links' centre is a pioneering venture allowing internationally renowned primatolo-gists from top Scottish universities the chance to carry out detailed studies of the animals while the zoo is caring for them.

This non-invasive, observational research will greatly enhance our knowledge of the behaviour of these fascinating animals.

The new centre will provide all that is best for the animals and members of the public will be able to see all that is going on. All who visit will be educated and informed and, in addition, be able to see how good science operates for the benefit of the animal kingdom.

Chimpanzee (IUCN status: Endangered)

How times have changed since the days of chimps' tea parties and one particular favourite at Edinburgh Zoo, a chimpanzee called Philip. He was donated to the zoo in 1933, already having developed a fondness for cigarettes and alcohol. The object of much observation and interest, such behaviour would no longer be tolerated. Research into the needs of such an animal has changed our thinking and our entire approach to how best to meet the behavioural needs of these intelligent animals.

Research within the zoo has always been an important part of its activities. In any one year the park can host as many as 50 research students and scientists from a dozen or more academic and scientific institutions. The areas of study vary from looking at animal behaviour and welfare, nutrition, psychology and physiology to all aspects of veterinary science.

As the zoo is developing, this important research aspect of its work is constantly evolving. Good observational studies can do much to enhance the general understanding and welfare of the captive animals and also be of immense help to those working on conservation projects in the wild.

For visitors the antics and displays of the primates are likely to reward their own study. With such a variety on show, regular visitors often have their favourites. The monkey houses and enclosures are always a great attraction.

The buff-cheeked gibbon (*Nomascus gabriellae*) species is dichromatic, meaning that the males and females are different colours. The males are black with pale cheeks and the females are buff-coloured all over. Like all gibbons, their arms are much longer than their legs. The reason for this can be seen as they swing through their enclosure with marvellous agility, moving with great speed and precision as they hang from the ropes and trees.

Buff-cheeked gibbon (IUCN status: Vulnerable)

Monkeys are generally divided between the 'Old World' monkeys of Africa and Asia and the 'New World' monkeys of Central and South America. Old World monkeys have downward pointing nostrils and large pads on their bottoms, allowing them to sit (and sleep) comfortably on the ground. New World monkeys are generally arboreal, and some have prehensile tails for gripping branches. Generally, Old World monkeys carry their babies on their chests, while New World monkeys give them rides on their back. Such simple facts are what make animals so interesting to observe.

Howler monkeys (*Alouatta caraya*) are perfectly named, as can be heard if the visitor is nearby when they are calling to each other or 'defending' their territory. Noisiest at dawn, this species announce their presence with a sound that resonates through their forest home for up to three miles. The calls help each different troop avoid one another and so prevent territorial fights that sap energy and waste time that could be better spent eating or resting. Howlers consume about a kilo of food daily, eating a variety of vegetation. This low energy diet means that the animals then spend up to three quarters of the day conserving their energy by resting.

The monkey's prehensile tail is very strong and can be used like another arm or leg so it is a great help. Howler monkeys often hang from their tails, curled around a branch while they feed on fruit, leaves and flowers.

Gelada baboons (*Theropithecus gelada*) are interesting primates that live on the high mountain grasslands of Ethiopia, where their long hairy coats help protect them from very low night temperatures. To keep away from predators, they often sleep huddled together on craggy treeless cliffs.

The zoo currently has two brothers, Apollo and Aladdin, and hopes to receive some females in the future for a managed breeding programme.

Black howler monkey (IUCN status: Least Concern)

Gelada baboon (IUCN status: Near Threatened)

The beautiful Diana monkey (*Cercopithecus diana diana*) is named after the Roman goddess Diana, as the curving sweep of their white brow is said to resemble the shape of Diana's hunting bow. They are highly threatened in their native West Africa, mostly as a result of being hunted for the bushmeat trade. They are also considered a delicacy at wedding feasts.

Keepers at Edinburgh Zoo manage the international conservation programme for this species. This means that they are responsible to the whole of the world zoo community for ensuring that a healthy and genetically diverse population of this particular monkey is maintained, by arranging all the exchanges of individual animals around the world.

The first L'Hoest's monkey (*Cercopithecus lhoesti*) to be born in Scotland was a female called Semliki, in March 2002. She was joined the following year by a young brother. Animals will breed only when the conditions are right and it is always a good indication to zoo staff and visitors alike that the animals are content if they feed well, breed and look after their young.

Such breeding is, of course, especially important when animal species are under threat in the wild. If conditions are not right then quite simply the animals do not, or cannot, breed and the population does not maintain itself or grow. The L'Hoest's monkeys' wild habitat, the high montane forests of central Africa, is being depleted and they are also hunted for the bushmeat trade.

Edinburgh Zoo staff manages the European studbook for this threatened species, and also that of the Hamlyn's. The zoo's pair of Hamlyn's monkeys (*Cercopithecus hamlyni*), Shaba and Kenge, produced their first infant in January 2005. The keepers have named him Toseen.

Like the other guenons, this species has very distinctive facial markings, in this case a long thin white stripe, which extends from the forehead to the nose. The observant visitor will also notice that there are certain parts of the male's anatomy that are distinctly blue! Such vivid colouring is a bold advertisement announcing the male's sex and which helps suggest his virility to females.

Left Diana monkey (IUCN status: Endangered)

Right L'Hoest's monkey (IUCN status: Near Threatened)

Nature always has a purpose and the extraordinary variety of shapes and sizes, colours and textures found in the animal kingdom are some of the reasons a visit to the zoo can be so fascinating. Just as wonderful and interesting are the huge variations in lifestyle that individuals and groups of animals choose for themselves.

It is important that those interacting with and providing for the animals on a daily basis understand as much as they can about them.

In common with most good modern zoos, Edinburgh has a general policy of not interfering with the animals. Unless it is necessary they will not be much handled, if at all, and will be moved out of their most natural location or group only if there is a real need, for example for veterinary purposes.

The smallest monkeys in the world are in the Callitrichid family, including all the marmosets and tamarins, living in the rainforests of Central and South America. They have soft, silky fur and many have long fringes of hair on their heads or ears. Generally, only the dominant female in a group will breed, giving birth to twins, occasionally triplets. All the family members will help in rearing the infants, just handing them back to the mother for feeding.

Marmosets are gum feeders, and they have specially adapted lower incisors that enable them to gouge into tree bark to release the sap. Marmosets and tamarins have very sharp claws on their feet and hands (unlike most other primates which have nails), which are very useful for clinging to trees and branches and also for catching insect prey.

Goeldi's monkey (*Callimico goeldii*) is a tiny species that comes from the upper Amazon basin in South America, where they live in close family groups consisting mainly of male – female pairs and their young. They keep in contact with more than 40 different calls and use rapid eyelid and ear movements when they are close. As adults and babies have the same dense black hair, visitors have to look very carefully to see a baby clinging on to one of its parents.

Pygmy marmosets (*Callithrix pygmaea*), as the name implies, are one of the smallest primates in the world. They live in forests and bamboo thickets in Brazil, Ecuador and Peru.

A curled up animal could fit into a human hand. The maximum length of an adult, excluding its tail, is 15 cm and a baby weighs just 15 gm at birth. Older members of the marmoset troop provide for infant care after the first couple of weeks when the breeding male carries out care duties.

When babies are born in captivity it is always a great event. Keepers will monitor the pregnant female and do all that they can to ensure that the best possible and most natural conditions are provided for the birth. Once the young have emerged, it is important that they are carefully monitored, as not all animals are good parents. Much can go wrong and if it is thought appropriate – especially if the species is conservation-dependent – a baby may be removed from its parents and hand-reared. The keeper can take on the role of a caring member of the troop!

This is usually seen, however, as the second-best option and sometimes it is necessary to stand well back and let nature take its course. This does mean that babies can die from parental carelessness or neglect. If such things happen in the wild, then sometimes this must happen in the zoo.

That said, so much more is available to the animals, from attentive keepers to vets with modern medicines.

The cotton-top tamarin (*Saguinus oedipus*) is another little primate that has a 'helper' system of rearing offspring. If there are babies in the group, visitors will see that all the adults help out; carrying them on their backs, and passing them from one to another with great care.

The species is one of the most endangered in the world. It is found only in the tropical rainforest and dry thorn savannah in northern Colombia. The main threat is the loss of their habitat for human settlement and agriculture, but also they are sold for the pet trade.

It's easy to see why the golden-headed lion tamarin (*Loentopithecus chrysomelas*) has its name. It has a splendid mane of golden hair that stands out from the black hair that covers the rest of its body, apart from its hands and the end of its tail, which are also bright orange-gold.

Seriously threatened in the rainforests of Brazil, Edinburgh's tamarins are part of a global conservation programme.

Left Goeldi's monkey (IUCN status: Near Threatened)

Right Golden-headed lion tamarin (IUCN status: Endangered)

Overleaf Pale-headed saki (IUCN status: Least Concern)

There is another group of primates that are included in the zoo's collection. Lemurs are not monkeys, but belong to a more primitive group of primates called prosimians. There are over 20 species of lemur, all living on the island of Madagascar, east of Africa, where they have evolved in isolation over millions of years. They vary greatly in size, habitat and diet but all species of lemur are under serious threat as a result of deforestation, pollution and hunting. Conservation programmes run by zoos and wildlife parks are the only hope of survival for many of this wonderful group of animals.

The blue-eyed black lemur (*Eulemur macaco flavifrons*) comes from the north coast of Madagascar. This species is dimorphic – the genders showing different colours – the males are entirely black, and the females are much paler, with a brownish back, white under parts and white ear tufts. However, they both have blue eyes. They eat mostly fruit and flowers, but also insects and they are mostly active at night when certain flowers open up to reveal their nectar.

The broad-nosed gentle lemurs (*Hapalemur simus*), are threatened mostly by loss of habitat, but also being hunted for food. Those in Edinburgh's collection are a living example of co-operation between zoos. The animals are on loan from Paris Zoo and are being looked after on a temporary basis while that zoo is being redeveloped.

It is important that animals are relocated to places where they will receive consistently good and expert care, and before any species is put elsewhere, very careful checks are made that suitable conditions can be maintained by the new host. In this, and many other of its activities, Edinburgh Zoo complies with guidelines laid down by the British and Irish Association of Zoos and Aquariums, in this case the Animal Transactions Policy.

Edinburgh Zoo's major redevelopment plans are designed to give minimal disruption to the animals and to the visitor experience.

Broad nosed gentle lemur
(IUCN status: Critically Endangered)

Ring-tailed lemur (IUCN: Vulnerable)

Where possible, the animals are moved around the park and into suitable new enclosures. After a very short time they settle in to their new territory and the vestige of smells from the previous occupants can often provide some extra interest and stimulation.

Sometimes it is kinder to transport an individual or group to another zoo where the welfare of the animal can be best served. Regular zoo visitors can miss a favourite animal because of this, but where the animals have a need then this is always top of the list of priorities.

The most common, and certainly one of the most popular, of all the lemur species is the ring-tailed lemur (*Lemur catta*). They live in large family groups, led by a dominant female. Younger females will stay in the group, but the males will have to leave to join new groups, and our keepers work hard to ensure they replicate this social structure as closely as possible, often moving males on to other collections.

Ring-tailed lemurs use their tails to help find each other, waving them like flags when walking through long grass or thick vegetation.

On sunny days, especially in the early morning, visitors may be lucky enough to see them sitting on their haunches, with their arms wide spread, sunbathing!

The Alaotran gentle lemur (*Hapalemur griseus alaotrensis*) is said to look like a small brown teddy bear. They are amongst the most endangered of all the lemur species, mostly as a result of habitat loss (their reed beds are being chopped down), but also they are hunted for food and the pet trade.

In their enclosure the keepers have ingeniously used ropes to recreate their reed-beds of Lake Alaotra. By replicating their natural wild habitat, the keepers are encouraging the animals to give full exercise to their natural behaviours. Even patterns of light and movement can be recreated in such a way to help the animals feel quite at home.

Visitors can walk though the red ruffed lemur (*Varecia variegata rubra*) enclosure, and may be lucky enough the see them climbing

Red ruffed lemur (IUCN status: Critically Endangered)

the ropes above their head. Such enclosure design has been developed to give visitors the extra excitement of feeling immersed in the animals' habitat. And it appears that, just so long as they are not approached or touched, the lemurs are quite happy to share their living space. Should they feel any alarm they will make it very clear through a series of calls. Researchers have noticed that lemurs have different calls to signal danger from above or from the ground.

Ruffed lemurs are the most arboreal of the lemurs, so on sunny days they will be seen high up in their bamboo play-frames, but if it's raining then it is far more likely that they will be seen indoors.

Red ruffed lemurs spend a lot of time grooming themselves and each other, using

their lower teeth and a specially adapted claw on the second toe of their hind foot.

The aye-aye (*Daubentonia madagascariensis*) is a fascinating prosimian from Madagascar that was thought to be extinct until it was re-discovered in 1957. Since then a number of small captive breeding colonies have been established. They are being carefully studied and it is quite possible that at some time individuals may be re-introduced into suitable wild habitats. The aye-aye is one of the most endangered mammal species on the island of Madagascar as they are often killed by the local people, who believe them to be bad omens.

Aye-ayes are the only primate known to use echo-location to find their prey. They tap with their specially extended middle finger on the trunk of a tree, listening for the hollow spaces where they will find the grubs. Once the food is located, they gnaw the bark to get at it with their especially thin finger.

The nocturnal life that aye-ayes lead presents a bit of a problem to a zoo that wants to give its visitors every opportunity to see and experience the animals. Because visiting usually takes place only during the main day-light hours, this can only be possible if night and day are reversed for the animals, using artificial lighting to illuminate their usual hours of darkness and very low levels of light in an enclosed space during visiting hours.

Because of the very special nature of this endangered species, Edinburgh Zoo staff felt that they wanted to gain much more experience of the animals before they displayed them in this way. Consequently visitors see them, if at all, sleeping during the day as they would naturally in the wild.

Once again this emphasises the absolute rule that it is the welfare of the animals that must take precedence.

Aye-aye (IUCN status: Endangered)

ON THE HOOF

One of the glories of the Edinburgh Zoo site is that the hill, often a burden to those walking up it, enables the imaginative building of viewing platforms out over some of the enclosures. Nowhere is this better demonstrated than at the African plains, where visitors can stroll along an elevated walkway to a viewing platform that gives complete 360-degree sight of the large open enclosure that is home to a mixed group of hoofed animals, or hoofstock, as they are often called.

Hoofed animals, known as ungulates, are divided into two groups – all decided by the number of toes on their front or back feet. Those with an odd number of toes are called perissodactyls, and these include zebras, horses, rhinoceroses and tapirs (the latter having four toes on their front feet and three on their hind feet). They are all herbivores, meaning that they eat only plants.

Those with an even number of toes are called artiodactyls, which includes hippopotamuses, pigs, giraffes, camels, cattle, deer and antelope. All of them are herbivores, except the pig family that are omnivores, meaning that they will eat almost anything. Many of these animals are prey species for carnivores, so they have adapted to be alert and speedy.

In the past (and still in some foreign zoos) hoofstock could be fed to the big cats when they were at the end of their useful life – providing food much as they would in the wild. Such are the health and safety regulations, and the need for following strict procedures that include animals having to be slaughtered in a registered abattoir, this is no longer the case in this country.

As with all of the animals in the zoo, there tends to be a moving population among the hoofstock in the zoo and animals come and go

according to the needs of the species as well as the individual animals. Over the years, Edinburgh Zoo has been particularly successful in the breeding and rearing of many of these hoofed species and keepers are keen to remain in the forefront of good welfare and husbandry.

As a species' status in the wild changes for the worse, the zoo will seek to take on the task of looking after its more long-term interests, usually by participating in a managed conservation programme, co-ordinated by a studbook keeper based in a European zoo.

Many of the hoofstock animals are suitable for exciting mixed displays, but such a feature is not without its problems. The African plains enclosure, famed for its mixture of species, has in the past caused some headaches for keepers. Not all animals get on well all the time, even if they are not apparently naturally vicious towards each other. Seasonal behaviour can also cause problems, with smaller animals sometimes being vulnerable to being trampled if they're in the way of a rutting stag, for example, so the staff are constantly on the look out for any behaviour that suggests the animals would be better separated.

Such problems can be overcome by clever enclosure design. For example, in the bongo enclosure there is an apparent mixture with red river hog. It is a bit of an optical allusion, however, as these two species are in fact separated, but with invisible moats and ditches designed in such a way that visitors have to look quite hard to see them.

The Eastern bongo (*Tragalaphus eurycerus isaaci*) is slightly larger than its West African counterpart, but they have the same striking coat of deep chestnut red marked with between 10 and 15 vertical white stripes. It is believed that their horns, which appear in both males and females, are sloped backwards to help them travel more easily through dense

Previous page Warthog (IUCN status: Lower Risk)

rainforests. The Eastern bongo is found only in Kenya, and is much rarer than its western counterpart.

The red river hog (*Potamochoerus porcus*) is a striking member of the pig family that enjoys wallowing in the rivers and swamps of the tropical rainforest of West Africa and the Congo Basin. They live in large, social groups, led by a dominant male. The zoo's male, Butler, was born in Rotterdam Zoo and the two females are Bonnie and Belle – sisters who came from Landau Zoo in Germany. Their part of the enclosure is something of a mess, thanks to their natural use of their strong snouts to root for food.

The Hamlyn's monkeys in the trees above and alongside these two species help nicely to tell the story of their wild habitat where all three might be seen together in a woodland clearing in Africa.

Left Eastern bongo (IUCN status: Endangered)
Below Red river hog (IUCN status: Lower Risk)

The African plains paddock currently contains a number of animals, among the most important of which is the Grèvy's zebra (*Equus grevyi*). This is an endangered species with which the zoo is involved both in Edinburgh and in their native habitat in Kenya and Ethiopia.

This zebra species was hunted almost to extinction in the twentieth century for its beautiful coat. It now faces habitat loss and competition for water with neighbouring humans. Before a zoo can take on a breeding programme they have to keep a group of bachelor males for five years before introducing a female. This enables the keepers to learn about the husbandry of these animals, ensuring their proper care. Most of the males are then moved away, leaving one stallion, and females are introduced. Stallions will mate from the age of about seven.

The present herd comprises the male, Chris, two adult females, Francesca and Emily, and two juveniles, Olivia and Daniel, born in 2001 and 2005 respectively. Not only are these delightful animals to watch as they canter around the plains, but they are also useful for helping to tell the story of our conservation work with their counterparts in the wild.

With a constantly developing Conservation Strategy, support for *in situ* conservation (that is, work in the wild) happens in a number of different but related ways. Enshrined in the strategy document and in practice is the fundamental principle that the Royal Zoological Society of Scotland works in partnership with other organisations, and does not attempt to 'reinvent the wheel'. As with so many other aspects of conservation, collective action is always more effective than 'going it alone'.

Every year, the Society provides funding, expertise and other resources to a number of carefully selected conservation projects around

Left Grèvy's zebra (IUCN status: Endangered)

the world, almost all of them linked to *ex situ* projects with animal species at Edinburgh Zoo.

Since the launch of the first strategy the RZSS has provided many hundreds of thousand pounds towards a huge variety of projects and this is a sum that is being continually added to from profits from events, donations from the safari bus, cash from volunteer-run activities and from public giving.

Currently there are two funding categories: a project facilitation grant and long-term funded conservation projects.

The first category is aimed at smaller projects, usually bound within short three-month time spans, and mostly carried out by under- or post-graduate students taking part in ecology, conservation biology and education-based university expeditions. These grants have, in the past, provided essential training opportunities to biologists as well as gathering important new information on species in their natural habitats. In recent years, this funding has enabled students and keepers to travel to places as diverse as the Falkland Islands, Kenya and south east Asia in pursuit of these studies, with tangible benefits for the wild populations.

Long-term conservation projects are aimed at clearly identified conservation action. One such principal conservation project in the wild is the programme for Grèvy's zebra in northern Kenya and southern Ethiopia. The Grèvy's zebra project is addressing a number of factors that have led to the dramatic decline of this species. Adapted to a semi-arid habitat, the animals are found in the dry mountainous regions of Samburu in Kenya and at fragmented sites in Ethiopia.

These animals need constant access to water and this places them in direct competition with man. Local communities rely on cattle and sheep grazing for their livelihoods, and zebras will not approach watering sites if people and livestock are present. This has a particular impact on females with young foals.

One of the objectives of the project is to establish sustainable water management systems that meet the needs of wildlife as well as the local people.

As well as water management schemes, community education and training programmes can help offset threats to wildlife. Education and other work with local partners takes in firearms control and eco-tourism initiatives, to encourage sustainable use of the environment that sees the value of the wildlife without putting it under undue pressure.

There is little doubt that *in situ* conservation work is often more about people than about the animals. It is vital work, for with no natural habitat the animals just cannot thrive.

Zebras (and all other members of the horse family) move on a single 'toe' or hoof, whereas antelope and deer are often referred to as 'cloven-hoofed' although in truth they have two separate digits, not one split into two, as the phrase would suggest.

Both deer and antelope are herbivores, either grazing on grassland or browsing on trees.

They are usually shy, very agile and are always on the look out for predators. They have to rely on their keen senses and their ability to run very fast in order to escape.

There are a variety of deer and antelope in the park and each species offers something different and of interest. The pudu (*Pudu puda*) is a tiny deer from Chile and Argentina that is most active in the early morning and late afternoon, when they go searching for leaves, twigs, buds, fruit and seeds. They can jump, stand on their hind legs to reach higher leaves and run in zigzag lines when they're frightened.

The zoo has done well in breeding this species, but there is a great problem of infant mortality due to respiratory problems. As this is happening elsewhere, much careful research is being carried out in the hope that this might someday be overcome.

Another little deer is the Reeves' muntjac (*Muntiacus reevesi*) from east Asia. Introduced into Britain in the eighteenth century by the Duke of Bedford to adorn his park, some of the animals escaped and they are now quite widespread in the wild.

Siberian musk deer (*Moschus moschiferus*) and lesser Malayan chevrotains (*Tragulus javanicus*) – which are also known as mouse deer – have features that separate them from other deer. Long upper canine teeth, for example, replace antlers and are used by the males for fighting. The musk deer secretes musk from its groin during the mating season and this is much in demand for the perfume industry.

Left Pudu (IUCN status: Vulnerable)

Right Siberian musk deer (IUCN status: Vulnerable)

Far right Kirks's dik-dik (IUCN status: Lower Risk)

Once again a human vanity can be the cause of endangering a species.

A sub-species of our more common red deer is the Bactrian wapiti (*Cervus elaphus bactrianus*) from Kazakhstan. With a migration range that covers four eastern European countries, it has suffered from differing laws in each one. Needless to say, the wapiti are blissfully unaware of these different laws, but it has left them vulnerable to over-hunting in some areas. It is heartening to note that recently all four countries have come together and agreed to a common protection plan, so the future for wapiti is looking much brighter.

Telling the difference between deer and antelope is not a great problem; the clue is in the horns. Deer grow antlers, which are shed and re-grown every year, whereas antelopes have horns that grow to their full extent and then stay more or less the same throughout their adult life. In many antelope species, the females have horns exactly the same as the males, but in deer the females usually have much smaller antlers or none at all.

The Kirk's dik-dik (*Madoqua kirkii*) is an antelope named after its alarm call. Those in Edinburgh are very nervous beasts and although it was planned to introduce them into the mixed enclosure near to the painted hunting dogs, this has not been possible so far. Keepers are constantly learning by observation about the animals' particular needs and it is still possible that at some time in the future they may be able to provide suitable hiding places that would encourage these nervous animals to feel secure.

The Japanese serow (*Nemorhaedus crispus*) is a goat-like antelope that lives in wooded hillsides and conifer forests in, as its name suggests, Japan. It seems to have quite a slow, clumsy gait, but it is very surefooted when walking on the steep rocky slopes that characterise its usual habitat. They establish regular paths, resting spots and places for defecation and mark their territory with secretions from glands situated just in front of their eyes.

When they are at odds with their fellows, they chase each other and can inflict nasty injuries using their sharp horns to stab an opponent.

This species is ideally suited to the conditions found in Edinburgh as is another species, the Chinese goral (*Nemorhaedus goral arnouxianus*). They are closely related and will often share the same habitat, but the gorals tend to live on the steeper, more barren slopes.

Gorals are seen to be half true antelope and half true sheep and goat. More heavily built than similarly sized antelopes, nevertheless they can move very fast. It has been observed that their hoofs have already left the spot before the rocks they dislodge have begun to move!

Like all Bovidae ruminants, the goral has a four-chambered stomach and it regurgitates partly digested food for chewing again as cud. The food can take up to four days to be digested.

Another ruminant from mountainous areas in China that can be found within the zoo park is the Mishmi takin (*Budorcas taxicolor taxicolor*). This animal has a place in mythology as it is thought that the 'Golden Fleece', the treasure sought by Jason and the Argonauts, came from a takin. Certainly its dense yellow to brown hair gives such an impression.

They tend to feed most in the early morning and late afternoon, taking regular paths to feeding and resting places. For such a large animal they are surprisingly good at camouflaging their whereabouts by lying low in the dense bamboo thickets, pressing their body into the ground and pushing out their necks to achieve as low a profile as possible.

A sharp cough is used as an alarm call, and one such noise can cause the complete herd of up to one hundred animals to flee.

Another herd animal, the scimitar-horned oryx (*Oryx dammah*) was once common throughout the Sahara desert. This magnificent antelope has been hunted to the edge of extinction for its horn and the zoo is very pleased to have participated in a successful

Left Chinese goral (IUCN status: Endangered)

Top right Mishmi takin (IUCN status: Endangered)

Bottom right Lechwe (IUCN staus: Lower Risk) and scimitar-horned oryx (IUCN status: Extinct in the Wild)

Overleaf Southern white rhinoceros (IUCN status: Near threatened)

breeding and reintroduction programme, called Operation Oryx. In 1985, three of Edinburgh's oryx, along with others from zoos in England, were returned to Tunisia, where they had been extinct since 1906.

The Bactrian camel (*Camelus bactrianus*) has two humps – the most obvious difference from the dromedary camel that has just one. Camels are superbly adapted to their harsh living environment. They have a hump filled with fat (not water as is often mistakenly believed) to supply them with food when it is otherwise scarce, a thick coat to keep them warm at night, a large body area to keep them cool during the day, and several features to keep out the sand, including very thick eyelashes and an upper lip which curls over the lower one.

The Bactrians' long, shaggy coats help them withstand the freezing temperatures in their native Mongolia and China, sometimes as low as –30°C.

The zoo's Bactrian family comprises father Khan, who came from Chester Zoo, mother Holly, who came from Whipsnade Wild Animal Park, and daughters Caramel, born in Whipsnade in 2003, and Khara who was born at Edinburgh Zoo in June 2004. Although many such animals elsewhere are somewhat domesticated those in Edinburgh are left very much to their own devices in order that they maintain their wild qualities.

Left Bactrian camel foal
Below Bactrian wapiti
(IUCN status: Vulnerable)
and Bactrian camels
(IUCN status: Critically Endangered)

Many of the hoofstock animals have to be managed for their own and the keepers' safety. While trying never to make pets of the animals, keepers will spend time with them, positively reinforcing behaviour that enables good husbandry. It might be, for example, that individuals will be fed inside so that, when needing to come in, they can be easily encouraged to do so. Training an individual to stand still or lie down is hugely helpful when veterinary attention is required.

All invasive veterinary procedures have an element of risk, so if the animal can be approached without having to be sedated then this can only be a good thing. A familiar keeper doing familiar things can help keep an animal calm when it is necessary and will often prevent the individual from rushing around and harming itself by hitting obstacles in its way.

Hippopotamuses are just not interested in doing things for food rewards, yet despite being a very aggressive animal, Edinburgh Zoo keepers have developed excellent husbandry for the pygmy hippopotamuses (*Hexaprotodon liberiensis*) in their care. Over the years some 12 youngsters have been bred and successfully reared. One very special baby was successfully hand-reared in 1993 by the staff at Edinburgh Zoo, only the second time this had been achieved in Britain. The keepers had to stay up with her round the clock for several days, and they called her Cleo, short for Cleopatra, because she was taught to suckle by being bathed in milk.

Unlike the much larger common hippos, which are very social and live in large herds, pygmy hippos are solitary and prefer their own company. So the current female, Leah, and her infant, Ellen, born in January 2005, are quite content on their own until the right mate is found to join them in the breeding programme for this threatened species.

Above Pygmy hippo (IUCN status: Vulnerable)
Right Malayan tapir (IUCN status: Vulnerable)

On sunny days, a whitish creamy secretion can be seen on their skin. It is a natural and very effective sun cream!

The southern white rhinoceros (*Ceratotherium simum simum*), although the least endangered of all the remaining rhino species, is still hunted for its horn which is mistakenly believed to have magical medicinal and aphrodisiac powers. The horn is also used to make ceremonial dagger handles. The zoo's famous female, Umfolozi (known affection-ately as Floozie by her keepers), gave birth to a record-breaking 13 calves before she died in 2005. Many of these have gone on to help form conservation breeding groups around the world. The young male, Samson, came from Knowsley Safari Park in 2004 as company for Umfolozi and it is likely that another, more conservation-dependent type of rhino, will be introduced into the zoo park in the future.

Another animal that might seem like a 'living fossil' is the Malayan tapir (*Tapirus indicus*). These animals are mostly nocturnal, and their striking coat pattern – black at the front and rear, with a grizzled white or grey in the middle – on their pig-like body is believed to help them to hide well in the moonlit forest at night.

Aggressive and more difficult to care for than their more placid lowland cousins, it is hoped that the Edinburgh pair will begin breeding in the next couple of years, as part of a European conservation programme to protect this threatened species.

The babirusa (*Babyrousa babyrussa*) is an elusive and unusual member of the pig family found only on the islands of Sulawesi in south-east Asia. There it is being studied *in situ* by scientists from Edinburgh University who are also keen to observe those found in the zoo. The remarkable tusks seen on the zoo's male, Tolo, are used in the wild for fighting other males, although there is a local legend that they use them to hang from trees at night!

Warthogs (*Phacochoerus africanus*) are another pig with large tusks. They shelter and raise their young in burrows, so they have to be introduced to a mixed enclosure with some care. The warthog is the only pig adapted for grazing in grassland. In the growing season, it can be seen kneeling and nipping off the grass tips using its lips or incisor teeth and in the dry season it roots out underground stems using its toughened snout.

A relative of the camel is the vicuña (*Vicugna vicugna*) from South America, where it lives at a height of 3,600 to 4,800 metres. It has a prehensile, cleft upper lip that enables it to feed by selectively snipping off the perennial grasses on which it feeds. It delineates its territory mainly by leaving piles of dung. Research into such behaviours greatly helps those working with the animals to know just where to tread!

Babirusa (IUCN status: Vulnerable)

FEATHERED FRIENDS

Of all types of wildlife, we probably have most experience of birds. From the comfort of our own homes, whether in a built-up area or in the countryside, we can see a large range of bird species. From the tiny wren flitting in the garden hedge to huge birds of prey soaring over the motorway, we can enjoy a great variety.

Worldwide there are more than 9,000 known species of birds and they are the most widespread of animals, found on icebergs and in deserts, on and under water as well as on the ground and in the air.

On the whole birds in northern Europe can be comparatively dull in their plumage. The red breast of the robin or the rush of iridescent colour when a kingfisher dives for fish always gives an extra thrill.

Birds of all colours, shapes and sizes and from all parts of the world are found within the zoo at Edinburgh. Many of these are under threat, mostly as the result of man's impact on the environment. These threats can range from fishing twine in English rivers being swallowed by swans to the unsustainable fishing by factory ships in the southern Atlantic, which threatens penguins' traditional feeding grounds.

For at least one species, the Socorro dove (*Zenaida graysoni*), the zoo is one of the very few places that it can be seen, as it is extinct in the wild. Successfully bred within the park, some of these birds may well be among the first to be reintroduced into their natural habitat on the island of Socorro just off Mexico. It is likely that when the time comes, one of the bird keepers from the zoo will be part of the team that will fly out to the island to help with settling the zoo bred birds into their natural home.

A similar story can be told about Edinburgh Zoo's involvement with the Montserrat oriole (*Icterus oberi*). Listed by the World Conservation Union as Critically Endangered, there may be only 100 pairs remaining in the wild. Edinburgh Zoo is working with Jersey Zoo and others around the world to help save this species.

Volcanic eruptions on the Caribbean island of Montserrat between 1995 and 1997, and in 2001 and 2003, have brought this bird to the edge of extinction. Their habitats have been destroyed, and the resulting ash causes ill health and lack of prey insects for the surviving birds. Thus the small zoo populations are doing vital work in keeping and breeding these pretty, timid creatures that are seen as Montserrat's national bird.

Birds can be found throughout the zoo park and increasingly the enclosures are designed give a particularly good and unusual close-up view to the visitor. A glass wall on the side of the large enclosure for the Steller's sea eagles (*Haliaeetus pelagicus*), for example, means that they can be seen in flight or perching in all of their glory. Since they have been introduced into this particular enclosure, keepers have noted that their agile flying loops have built up their flight muscles and contributed greatly to their general fitness.

Left Steller's sea eagle (IUCN status: Vulnerable)

Right Socorro dove (IUCN status: Extinct in the Wild)

Previous page Great grey owl (IUCN status: Least Concern)

This huge and stunning bird, one of the largest of the eagle species, is declining in its wild populations because of habitat degradation, pollution, poisoning by lead shot and over-fishing (depriving it of its prey). In the wild in China, Russia, Japan, Korea and the United States it lives near rivers, lakes and freshwater marshes, which explains why the zoo's pair enjoy the gushing waterfall and pond in their aviary.

Still both quite young, it is hoped and expected that this pair of birds will breed within the next few years.

Uninterrupted views of the birds can be taken for granted when considering the penguin colony at the zoo. Two things contribute considerably to this: the glass windows allowing a view of their underwater swimming activities and the regular parades that some of the penguins enjoy outside of their enclosures and among the general public.

Penguins have been important to Edinburgh Zoo since 1914, the year after it opened, when the first gift of a penguin was made by the Salvesen Whaling Company on their return from an expedition to the south Atlantic. Ever since then, Edinburgh Zoo has led the way in learning about and caring for this fascinating bird, and our keepers regularly help to train penguin keepers from all over the world.

There are 18 species of penguin, all found in the southern hemisphere, ranging from the frozen wastes of Antarctica to the shores of Australia, South Africa and South America. None of them can fly because their ancestors moved from the air to the water around 100 million years ago. This is why there is no net over the penguin enclosure. They are excellent swimmers and have dense, oily feathers and a thick layer of fat underneath the skin to keep them warm in even the coldest waters.

The king penguin (*Aptenodytes patagonica*) is second in height only to the emperor penguin and has a deep golden-yellow splash of colour on its bill, head and upper chest. They live in rocky, snowy areas of the south Atlantic, including the Falklands. King penguins don't build nests, but they incubate the egg on top of their feet, insulated by a flap of skin. The female and male share the incubation of the egg as well as the later feeding of the chick.

Edinburgh Zoo was the first place in the northern hemisphere to see the successful hatching of a king penguin chick in 1919, and it has been dear to its heart ever since. Indeed, it has been adopted as the logo, and can be seen on all of the zoo's uniforms, signs and leaflets.

Also in the penguin enclosure there is a colony of small grey and white gentoo penguins (*Pygoscelis papua*). These are found widely throughout the Antarctic and its islands. They are the fastest swimming underwater bird, reaching speeds of 36 kilometres an hour when they are hunting for krill or fish.

Above Gentoo penguin
(IUCN status: Near Threatened)

Right Rockhopper penguin (IUCN status: Vulnerable)

Below King penguin chick
(IUCN status: Least Concern)

The female gentoo usually lays two eggs, although in the wild the second one rarely survives. Their nests are made carefully, using mostly pebbles, and these become like a currency for these active and acquisitive birds. Visitors to the zoo between February and April will see frequent stealing and redistribution of pebbles!

A third species kept in the zoo, rockhopper penguins (*Eudyptes chrysocome*) can be very aggressive towards other species, so they are looked after in a separate enclosure from the other penguins. Rockhoppers live on many of the rocky islands of the south Atlantic, and their name derives from their habit of jumping across very craggy ground with their two feet close together. They have a distinctive plumage of long yellow feathers on their brow, which they shake to attract a mate during the breeding season. They have small red eyes and an orange bill.

As has been mentioned, not all of the Royal Zoological Society of Scotland's work takes place in the zoo. Conservation work can often be best done in the wild – in the animals' natural habitat.

In the Falklands, where there is one of the most important breeding sites for many species of seabirds and mammals, the Society is working with Falklands Conservation to make sure that this vital site is maintained for the good of its non-human occupants.

A few months spent there by one of the zoo's penguin keepers contributed greatly to the local understanding of these animals. Having worked closely with the Edinburgh colony, she was able to share her knowledge with the local wardens, and confirm some of their interpretations of penguin behaviour. Needless to say, she also gained from the experience, and the care of the zoo population of penguins has benefited in turn since her return.

Many of the animals in the zoo are 'adopted' by supporters and there is one particularly special penguin, named Nils Olav, which is supported by the Royal Norwegian Guard. Every time this smart troop of soldiers performs at the Edinburgh Tattoo they come to visit him at the zoo and, in a special ceremony each time, they have promoted him up the ranks of their regiment. From his first outing as a lance corporal he now currently holds the rank of Colonel-in-Chief.

To celebrate their long association with the king penguins at Edinburgh Zoo, the Royal Norwegian Guard presented the zoo and the city of Edinburgh with a bronze statue of a king penguin in August 2005. Created by a renowned Norwegian sculptor, Oystein Bernhar Mobraten, it was presented by former members of the Guard in the presence of Nils Egelien who, as a young lieutenant, was the man who instigated the adoption following his visit in 1972. The sculpture was unveiled by the city's Lord Provost in a ceremony which marked the close collaboration between the Scottish and Norwegian people. There is another casting of the sculpture in the Guard's Oslo barracks that was unveiled by the King of Norway.

The pleasure of close contact with the animals in the zoo takes many forms. The sense of ownership by adoption means that regular visitors can make a beeline for their very own special animal and chart its life and progress with a degree of satisfaction, knowing that they are contributing to its upkeep and welfare

Others support the Society's overseas *in situ* conservation work, either directly with a valuable donation or through a proportion of their entrance ticket money and purchases in the zoo shops or catering outlets. All the proceeds from the zoo's commercial operations are used to support the Society's conservation and education objectives.

Often it is the daily education programme of animal talks and demonstrations that inspire such generosity. In these close encounters with the animals, visitors are excited and inspired by the sheer wonder of being in close proximity with living creatures demonstrating their natural behaviours.

There is nothing more spectacular than the flying demonstrations in the hilltop area of the zoo. Trained using positive reinforcement techniques, these great birds swoop and soar for the delight of all.

The birds in these displays are cared for in a slightly different way from others in the zoo. Necessarily they are handled a great deal and the small presentation team works with them, constantly maintaining a close relationship that is not the norm for the keepers in the main bird section. There the general approach is hands-off except when absolutely necessary for the welfare of the individual bird.

The great success of the public encounters with the animals is seen to be beneficial in all sorts of ways. A greater understanding and

Left Nils Olav reviews the Royal Norwegian Guard

Right Grey crowned crane
(IUCN status: Least Concern)

empathy can be engendered in an easy fashion when people are truly engaged and the education team in the zoo get constant feedback that this particular aspect of the work is both valued and valuable.

Perhaps the most enjoyed flying displays are those of the raptors.

Raptors, also known as birds of prey, include owls, eagles and hawks – all of which are excellent hunters. They are superbly equipped with sharp talons, hooked bills and strong senses of hearing, sight or smell to help them locate and kill their prey.

There are few things more full of wonder and excitement than to be just under the flight path of the silent Bengal eagle owl (*Bubo bubo*) that has been trained to fly above the heads of the unsuspecting visitors, chasing a morsel of food.

Other raptors to be found in enclosures around the park include the very popular great grey owls (*Strix nebulosa*), which sit silently hunched in the trees – occasionally flying down to feed, especially as dusk falls.

The great grey owl is much smaller than it looks. Underneath its generous covering of feathers it is about the same size as a tawny owl. Living in the dense forests of the northern hemisphere, with long winters and low light levels, it uses its excellent sense of hearing to help locate its prey – mostly voles and lemmings – even when they're under the snow.

Because we can see many raptors in the wild in our own country they tend not to look quite so extraordinary as do the some of the more exotic species from distant lands. In the zoo park there are some fabulous (in the true sense of that word) birds.

The grey crowned crane (*Balearica regulorum gibbericeps*), for example, is an amazing 'living fossil' of the crane family, an ancient bird group which goes back over 60 million years. Edinburgh has five adults in its Maji Mzuri

aviary, alongside the painted hunting dogs, where visitors may be lucky enough to see some of their marvellous displays of dancing, hopping and bowing, all part of their bonding and mating rituals.

This enclosure, offering a mixed collection of birds, provides a very natural context for their display and their proximity to mammals that would be fairly close to them in the wild extends the visitor's experience through this microcosm of the vast African habitat. The enclosures are designed to complement each other and are an indication of the direction in which the zoo planners hope to move in the future. More integrated groups of exhibits will be offered through the provision of a system of biomes throughout which the animals will be found in proximity to other species, just as they would in the wild.

Also within the Maji Mzuri aviary is the curious bird the hamerkop (*Scopus umbretta*). This water-loving African species has a hammer-shaped outline of the head, a blunt beak and backward-pointing tuft of feathers and its behaviour is fascinating.

It builds the largest nest of any bird and in the wild pairs may build as many as five in a season, though only one is used. This nest is used not only by the hamerkops, but by all sorts of other animals such as bees, snakes and mongooses that take up residence in the huge construction of twigs, grass and mud.

Von Der Decken's hornbill
(IUCN status: Least Concern)

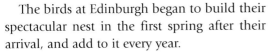

The birds at Edinburgh began to build their spectacular nest in the first spring after their arrival, and add to it every year.

Fantastic birds from other great continents are also to be found as visitors wander around the zoo.

The southern cassowary (*Casuarius casuarius*) is a large, strong and flightless bird that lives in the dense rainforests of northern Australia and Papua New Guinea. Here its droppings help to distribute fruit seeds, demonstrating in a strong way the importance of all birds to the eco-systems in which they live.

In common with another flightless bird, the ostrich, once the female cassowary has laid her eggs, she leaves (to look for a new mate) and the father incubates the eggs and looks after the chicks. It is hoped that the zoo's pair will breed before too long so that visitors will be able to see this amazing display of fatherly love.

From the craggy shores of Morocco and in Syria, the Waldrapp ibis (*Geronticus eremita*) is a critically endangered bird, with perhaps fewer than 100 left in the wild. At first glance, this is not one of the most attractive birds but, especially when the sun shines, visitors can see an amazing range of iridescent colours in its plumage.

Once found extensively throughout the freshwater wetlands of South America, the Chilean flamingo (*Phoenicopterus chilensis*) is now threatened by habitat degradation, due to mining and changes in land use, as well as the impact of tourism. After a gap of nearly 10 years, zoo staff were delighted when a flamingo chick was successfully hatched in the park in the summer of 2004.

Above Southern cassowary
(IUCN status: Vulnerable)

Below Waldrapp ibis
(IUCN status: Critically Endangered)

Overleaf Chilean flamingo
(IUCN status: Near Threatened)

Regrettably this chick did not reach maturity as a fox burrowed its way into the flamingo enclosure and took the young bird. Such is nature, but the keepers were quick to ensure that such a thing could not happen again by working on the perimeter of the enclosure. It is interesting to think that some of the barriers are to keep wild animals out and not in!

However, in some cases, access to some of the enclosures is not only permitted, it is even encouraged for visitors. Open to the elements, but covered with a mesh are a couple of ponds where a number of waterfowl species live and into which the general public has access.

Among those living here are Meller's duck (*Anas melleri*) which are unique to Madagascar. Like so many other species, this duck is threatened by changes to its natural habitat, particularly the deltas of the Mahavavy and Mangoky rivers, where there is increasing agricultural use for growing rice and other crops. Edinburgh Zoo is part of a European conservation programme to save this bird, which looks remarkably similar to our own mallard.

Above Chilean flamingo chick
(IUCN status: Near Threatened)

Below Madagascar teal (IUCN status: Endangered)

Like the Meller's duck, the Madagscar teal (*Anas bernieri*) is found only in wetland margins of western Madagascar, where there may be fewer than 1,000 birds left. Conservation efforts to save this and many other species are being co-ordinated by the Durrell Wildlife Conservation Trust at Jersey Zoo.

Many people like to walk through and even linger in these shady enclosures, quietly relishing the opportunity to sit and watch the gentle antics of these charming birds.

Another place where visitors can enjoy an uninterrupted encounter with birds is by the koala enclosure where they go through two doors to find themselves in the warmth of an interior set aside for birds from the Australian continent.

Here there are no real barriers, but the design is subtly engineered to ensure that the birds feel safe and untroubled by the passing visitors. Keepers have observed that entering this large room is like going into a library – everyone goes quiet. Something about the enclosure seems to engender a hushed respect. People are taken aback by their closeness to the birds and by the unfazed trust that they show.

Among the birds found here are the Victoria crowned pigeons (*Goura victoria*), quite unlike the Scottish pigeons found outside in the park. This species seems to be not in the least upset by the close presence of humans. In fact, they are so relaxed that within a very short time of taking up residence they were attempting to build a nest.

So many of the birds within the park may lack the glamour of their bigger neighbours, but their need to be in the zoo is usually just as important, if not more so.

The Bali starling (*Leucopsar rothschildi*) is one of the most endangered species on the planet, almost entirely due to illegal poaching for the pet trade. In 2001 only six birds were recorded living in the wild (on the north coast of Bali in Indonesia) but thankfully there are around 1,000 in captivity. Edinburgh Zoo is part of an international conservation programme to save this beautiful bird.

Only a couple of thousand of the thick-billed parrot (*Rhynchopsitta pachyrhyncha*) can now be found in its native Mexico, where logging for growing crops and drugs, as well as being hunted for the pet trade, has reduced its numbers drastically.

Again the zoo has successfully bred several chicks over the past few years as part of a managed European breeding programme.

Similarly, the red-fronted macaw (*Ara rubrogenys*) has its place in the zoo as there may be only a few hundred individuals left in the tiny area on the slopes of the Andes in east central Bolivia where this colourful parrot is found. It is mostly bright green, with blue primary feathers and very deep red plumage on its head and shoulders.

Right Victoria crowned pigeon
(IUCN status: Vulnerable)

Edinburgh Zoo is helping to fund an education programme with local people in Bolivia to help raise awareness of the importance of this lovely bird.

Education is a hugely important part of the work of the Royal Zoological Society of Scotland, and the zoo and Wildlife Park help greatly in this process. A dedicated team of teachers work with the keepers and conservationists both in Scotland and overseas to inform both children and adults about the wonders of the natural world and the part that we all have to play in maintaining a proper balance.

The educational significance of the zoo is enormous and the work in this field, done by all its staff, has been at the heart of the Society since its early beginnings and for the nearly one hundred years of its existence. Good zoos can offer particular focus, support and enrichment for all sorts of educational activity.

Both formal for schools and colleges and informal with community programmes for all ages, the education process takes many forms. Class visits, talks, lectures, guided walks, overseas study tours and the like make the zoo a real centre for learning. Day conferences, like the successful Global Classroom series for secondary aged students, are hugely popular and a very effective way of engaging young adults in stimulating debate. The summer schools, which run for four weeks during the school holidays, are immensely successful, focusing on a different theme each year, and with many families making automatic bookings for the following year.

The zoo offers the chance to make all sorts of links between our own lives and those from other cultures and countries, using the animals as the catalyst. 'Look deep into nature,' said Albert Einstein, 'and then you will understand everything better.' Ever innovative and willing and able to be flexible, the education work is much used and well received.

Edinburgh Zoo's educational mission statement is 'to inspire in our visitors an understanding of the value, the complexity and the fragility of the natural world by fully utilising the educational potential of our unique variety of living animals'. That mission is fulfilled daily, thanks to the work of a well-informed and enthusiastic group of staff and volunteers, all of whom are keen to pass on their own enthusiasms and passions for the animals and the zoo.

Red-fronted macaw (IUCN status: Endangered)

COOL CREATURES

Warm-blooded humans seem to have something of a problem with many of the ectothermic animals. There appears to be something about certain cold-blooded species – snakes, alligators, newts and toads – that causes upset and many would prefer not to visit the reptile house at the zoo.

It could be argued, of course, that it's entirely rational to fear animals which contain toxins or sharp teeth. But of course the animals are safely contained and those visitors who can face up to these fears are sure to be thrilled by the variety of animals on show. Furthermore, there is also sometimes a chance to meet and handle a beautiful boa as part of the regular 'animal encounters' educational experiences on offer. There need be no worries about it attempting to constrict anyone, as it is sure to have been well fed before it comes out to meet the public!

Reptiles are vertebrates with a backbone. They are ectothermic (cold-blooded) which means that they get their body temperature from the environment around them, so almost all reptiles live in warm regions of the world, either temperate or tropical.

There are many more reptile species than mammals (of which there are around 4,600). Amongst the reptiles, there are currently estimated to be 2,500 species of snake, 3,000 lizards, more than 250 species of tortoise and 21 crocodilians (which include crocodiles and alligators).

Snakes are formidable animals. They are highly developed predators that can kill and eat other creatures ranging from ants to antelopes. They use well-developed senses to find their prey, which they then subdue by using constriction or a poisonous bite. The food is not chewed and even very large animals can be swallowed whole because of loosely

connected bones in the skull that allow the jaws to be opened very wide.

Only about one in ten snakes is venomous and it comes as a relief to note that only a small number of these are dangerous to humans.

As an alternative to using venom, some snakes are constrictors – wrapping themselves around their prey and swallowing them. Among the constricting snakes that can be found in the zoo is D'Albert's python (*Liasis albertisii*). It lives in the rainforests of south east Asia and Australia, so is vulnerable to any damage to its environment. The iridescent scales on this snake make it a particularly colourful occupant of the reptile house.

On the whole, the huge variation of markings on snakes serve as camouflage and it is often very difficult to spot them as they lie still and silent in the sand, on rocks or wrapped around branches in their enclosures.

Previous page Standing's Day gecko (IUCN status: Vulnerable)

The Madagascar tree boa (*Sanzinia madagascariensis*) adults are greenish-brown in colour, but when the babies are first born they are bright red. Successful births have meant that the zoo has been able to participate well in the European conservation breeding programme for this species.

This interesting snake is declining in the wild, mostly as a result of deforestation and mining in Madagascar, but also because it is caught for the pet trade.

Left D'Albert's python (IUCN status: Not Listed)

Below Madagascar tree boa
(IUCN status: Vulnerable)

While many people abhor reptiles, some want to keep them as pets. Many snakes, lizards, tortoises and turtles are comparatively easy to keep in captivity and their exotic qualities appeal to some. Unfortunately not all of those who take the animals as pets are scrupulous about how they are acquired and there is a large illicit international trade in some of the more rare species.

Some zoo animals come by way of HM Customs and Excise after they have been confiscated at sea and air ports. Apart from the ethical problems of taking animals from the wild, there are also serious welfare concerns as many of the animals are in a very sorry state, having been taken from their natural habitat by people who do not really know how they need to be treated. Animal keepers at Edinburgh Zoo have developed great skill in the rehabilitation

of animals which have been brought in from customs seizures very close to death.

The reptile house contains members of four reptile types: snakes, lizards and their relatives, chelonians (reptiles with a shell, such as tortoises, turtles and terrapins) and crocodilians.

There is not space for the larger and more spectacular species of crocodile or alligator, but the zoo does have a pair of West African dwarf crocodiles (*Osteolaemus tetraspis*). Although small, they do demonstrate the attraction of this apparently fierce animal.

They lie as still as stones in their pool, with their eyes just above water level, allowing them to swim silently and unseen towards their prey in the wild. With the nostrils, eyes and ears lying in a line, a crocodile can keep ninety five per cent of its body beneath the surface yet still breathe and remain alert to any riverbank activity.

Lucky zoo visitors might find the female caring for eggs on a particularly messy nest that belies the fact that crocodiles are extremely gentle and protective of their young. Just before they are due to hatch, the hatchlings 'chirp' to their mother from within the egg, prompting her to help them emerge. In the wild she would then carry the young in her mouth, a few at a time, to a quiet spot in a nearby river where they will take their first swim.

The rapid sideways swipe of the jaw as a crocodile takes its prey is one of the iconic images of wildlife films. Such sights are a reminder that many of the animals in the zoo – especially poisonous reptiles and amphibians – need very careful handling. There are clear safety protocols for dealing with all of the animals, and in the reptile house there is often a need for extra precautions.

There is a rule that there should always be at least two people when in the presence of a dangerous animal. Consequently if anything untoward does happen then there is somebody else to help deal with the situation and to ensure the safety of both human and animal. Gloves must be worn when handling creatures that are poisonous (that is, toxic) or venomous (this is when the poison is injected, as with a snake bite).

Experience is a hugely important extra factor, as this helps with the reading and anticipation of an animal's behaviour. If it is known what an animal might do, then keepers can always be on the look out for signs of dangerous activity. Another important factor is knowledge of the facts about the animals in a zoo situation. While great care will always be taken, it helps the keepers greatly to know that in captivity poisonous frogs lose about fifty per cent of the toxicity in the oil on their skin with each generation.

Left Learning about snakes helps to overcome fear

Below Beaded lizard (IUCN status: Vulnerable)

Should a keeper be poisoned by one of the animals – fortunately a very rare occurrence – there is a well-prepared procedure that is followed for warning the hospital about the nature of the problem. The medical staff in the local hospitals have special incident sheets telling which are the most effective antidotes to use when a patient from the zoo arrives in the clinic.

However, one of the reptiles in the zoo's collection poses a particular health and safety problem, as there is no known antidote to its poison.

The beaded lizard (*Heloderma horridum*) is named after the spots and stripes on its bumpy skin that appear like beads. It is one of only two poisonous lizards in the world (the other being the gila monster). The lizard has a wide appetite, eating eggs, birds, small mammals and even other reptiles. Although it looks slow, it can move very fast while hunting its prey, so the keepers are really careful when in contact with the animals, which came to Edinburgh from Glasgow Zoo when it closed in 2003.

The reptile house is also the place to find some spectacular amphibians. Visitors can see one of nature's special ways of warning that an animal is poisonous epitomised by some remarkable species of frogs.

Frogs are amphibians, along with toads, salamanders and newts. The word 'amphibian' comes from the Greek meaning 'a being with a double life' because, after hatching from eggs, amphibians start their life in water (such as frog tadpoles) breathing with gills, then change into land animals which breathe with lungs.

Those that are poisonous are amongst the most vividly coloured on earth.

The amazing blue poison arrow frog (*Dendrobates azureus*) lives only in the warm humid forests of Surinam in South America, where it is vulnerable to forest fires and hunting for the pet trade. Its bright blue colour acts as a warning to predators (like birds and snakes) to let them know that it is toxic.

Native American Indians use the poisonous secretions from their skin to coat the tips of their arrows when they go out hunting for deer and other prey. In 1992 keepers at Edinburgh Zoo were the first in Europe to breed this frog, and froglets have since been sent to several zoos around the world to start new conservation breeding groups.

It's easy to see how the strawberry poison arrow frog (*Dendrobates pumilio*) got its name: it is coloured orangey-red, and dotted with small black spots. Like all poison arrow frogs, the fathers are very involved in the care of the eggs and the young tadpoles, carrying them on their backs to the water, and sometimes separating them to avoid them eating each other!

Above Strawberry poison arrow frog (IUCN status: Least Concern)

Left Blue poison arrow frog (IUCN status: Vulnerable)

Above Phantasmal poison arrow frog
(IUCN status: Endangered)

The tiny brown Trinidad stream frogs (*Colostethus trinitatus*) are much more difficult to see than their brightly coloured cousins, but if they cannot be seen, then they almost certainly will be heard as they have a really loud call.

As well as on the island of Trinidad, they are also found on Tobago, but their numbers are very vulnerable to deforestation. Edinburgh Zoo keepers have successfully bred several generations of this threatened frog, and sent them to many other zoos.

It is strange to think that turtles, tortoises and terrapins, with their distinctive shells, are among the oldest of creatures on Earth. They have changed very little in the 250 million years since their ancestors, found in fossil records.

The terrestrial species are known as tortoises and those that live in fresh water are usually known as terrapins. The term turtle was traditionally reserved for the marine species, but now scientists tend to refer to all members of the order as turtles.

Edinburgh Zoo has a number of different species, including the African spurred tortoise (*Geochelone sulcata*), a large member of the tortoise family that can be found along the southern edge of the Sahara desert from Senegal in the west, across central Africa and into the Middle East.

It is facing decline due to over-grazing and desertification, but many African cultures believe that this tortoise is a mediator between men and the gods, so happily they are keen to help with conservation programmes to protect it.

As its name suggests, the pancake tortoise (*Malacochersus tornieri*) is very flat, with adults being fifteen centimetres in length but only three centimetres in height. Its extremely flexible shell allows it to squeeze into very narrow crevices in rocky outcrops, known as 'kopjes' in its native Kenya and Tanzania, to escape from predators and to avoid extremes of temperature. Edinburgh has been breeding this species successfully since 1999, when the zoo received the first individuals that had been seized as illegal imports by HM Customs and Excise.

The smallest and most endangered tortoise in the northern hemisphere, the Egyptian tortoise (*Testudo kleinmanni*) is found only along the desert coasts of north Africa and Israel.

Previous page African spurred tortoise
(IUCN status: Vulnerable)

Right Egyptian tortoise
(IUCN status: Critically Endangered)

It is particularly threatened by degradation of its habitat and the illegal pet trade, which continues despite an international ban. If these threats are not controlled, it is feared that this lovely animal may become extinct in the next 20 years.

Above Starred agama (IUCN status: Not Listed)

Many species of tortoise have been declining rapidly in numbers in the past 30 or so years and when it is considered that in some form or other they have been around for nearly 250 million years, it is not difficult to see the importance of supporting the various conservation programmes designed to raise awareness of the threat and to attempt to do something to stop this rapid decline.

Each year Edinburgh Zoo, in common with many other zoos around Europe, encourages support of particular conservation campaigns. Co-ordinated by the European Association of Zoos and Aquaria (EAZA), these campaigns raise both public awareness and money to carry out vital work to prevent the worst abuses of all sorts of species. In this way the zoo and its visitors can give direct and meaningful help to conservation work in the field. Funds raised go to existing projects, so there are no administration or start-up costs to divert the money raised, and all the projects are carefully selected and evaluated.

Over the past few years, these campaigns have effectively raised funds and awareness for a range of different species and habitats including tigers, great apes, Amazonian rainforests and British native species. In 2005, the zoo participated in the EAZA ShellShock campaign which highlighted the plight of turtles around the world and raised over €250,000 for projects in south east Asia, including areas affected by the tsunami at the end of 2004.

DOWN UNDER

Great excitement surrounded the arrival of two koalas (*Phascolarctos cinereus*) in the summer of 2005. The only ones in Britain at the time, they came from San Diego Zoo in California after much behind-the-scenes work to ensure the best possible welfare for these fascinating animals.

Nothing is taken for granted in the zoo world and, however high a particular establishment's reputation may be, many checks will be made and training given before a new species is sent from another zoo. Like many other animals at Edinburgh Zoo, this particular pair of animals was sent on a permanent loan basis. Outside of Australia, San Diego is the biggest holder and breeder of koalas and they have co-ordinated the managed breeding programme for this species, principally for American zoos, for many years.

Coming into the United Kingdom, the koalas have become part of the European managed programme, run by Duisburg Zoo in Germany. It is hoped that eventually a female or two will be introduced and breeding can take place.

With increasing problems for the wild population and mindful of the unique and fascinating quality of marsupials, the zoo staff felt that koalas would offer a special opportunity to tell something of the rich story of Australian habitat and wildlife.

San Diego's loan programme is very strictly run, along very similar lines to the Animal Transactions Policy laid down by the British and Irish Association of Zoos and Aquariums. Before agreeing to send the animals to Edinburgh, visits were arranged between the two zoos, so that the San Diego staff could share their wide and comprehensive knowledge of this species, and their particular

Previous page and facing page Koala (IUCN status: Near Threatened)

husbandry needs. Comprehensive guidelines were very strictly followed, even extending to such things as food preparation and storage.

Once the accommodation was sorted out, the transport was the next challenge. As with all animal moves, the conditions were clearly set out and followed to the letter, to ensure the safety of the animals and the travelling public, of course. One of the American keepers who was well known to the animals travelled with them (it is rumoured that each of the koalas had their own seat on the flight over!) and she stayed in Edinburgh until she was satisfied that they were settled.

Koalas have a very specialised diet, so plans had to be made for a range of eucalyptus branches and leaves to be available to give variety to their apparently simple diet. Some eucalyptus trees are especially being grown in the park in Edinburgh, but a fresh supply has been sourced from the south of England and the food is regularly shipped up to Scotland.

Found principally in the eucalyptus forests of Queensland, Victoria, New South Wales and parts of Southern Australia, the koala is now under a variety of threats. This includes habitat loss and frequent forest fires, but another major problem for the species is to do more directly with human beings as they are often hit by cars on roads and subject to dog attacks when they come down to the ground to move from one tree to another.

It is reckoned that there are fewer than 100,000 koalas are left in the wild, with several thousand being killed every year. Their legal or protection status varies from one State to another and many organisations are working in Australia to increase their legal status in places where less protection is offered.

Koalas are the national emblem of Australia. Their name comes from the Greek words *phaskolos* meaning a bag or pouch, and *arctos* meaning bear. In fact, they are not bears at all, but they are indeed pouched animals, or marsupials, like many of the mammals in Australia. The mother has a furry pouch on her lower abdomen, into which the tiny baby (no bigger than a bee) crawls just after it is born. And there it stays, suckling on her milk and well protected from all predators, until it is large enough to leave and fend for itself.

Koalas get all their food and water from the gum leaves of the eucalyptus tree, and they spend their entire lives sitting in these trees, only coming onto the ground to move to a different eucalyptus tree! They get so little energy from this diet that they have to spend up to 18 hours a day resting or sleeping, in order to conserve their energy.

Zoo staff therefore had to design an enclosure that would not only fulfil all the koalas' particular needs for eating and resting, but also make them visible to the visitors. Even dozing they can continue to delight if they can be seen, and their habit of wedging themselves securely into the fork of a tree branch is a great help as such places have been provided in clear view. The two koalas, young brothers named Chumbee (meaning Torpedo Bug) and Jannali (Moon), settled happily into this carefully-designed habitat and proved an immediate hit with the visitors.

Although they look very cuddly, koalas have very sharp claws at the end of their fingers, which enable them to get a very tight grip of the tree bark as they climb and rest. They also help the animals to strip the leathery leaves off the branches.

The way in which the whole of the koala exhibition area and enclosure has been designed is indicative of the way in which all good zoos seek to fulfil their mission of providing properly for the welfare of the animals while offering a chance for some scientific research and the education of visitors. This latter activity always includes attempting to give some sense of, and to elicit a commitment to, the conservation needs of the various habitats and species.

Unashamedly using the delightful koalas as a magnet to attract the visitor, within the general Australian exhibit in Edinburgh Zoo there is an offering of the interesting and fascinating stories surrounding koalas, marsupials and Australian wildlife in general. But the exhibit also, in line with the aims of the zoo's future plans, expands out and attempt to inform visitors about the habitat that these animals come from, the importance and diversity of the Eucalypt forests

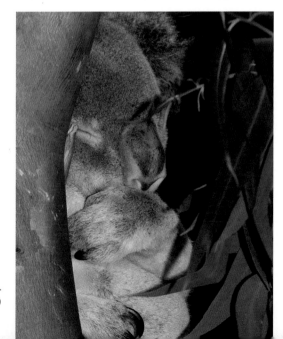

of Australia and of the variety of plant and animal life that are found within them.

Within this section can be seen a display of dung beetles (*Kheper aegyptiorum*), the only insect species exhibited in the zoo. Due to their nature, however, there is rarely much action to be seen!

Having been extensively studied and filmed we know what it is that makes these insects interesting, but they do seem to be an example of real life not imitating art. Living creatures left to their own devices can be infuriatingly unhelpful when visitors have travelled long distances for the purpose of observing them. It is important under such circumstances to remember that all of the animals in the collection are allowed to live their lives in the best and most natural conditions that can be provided and with a minimum of interference by humans. If they choose to hide away, then that is why hiding places have been provided.

In the case of the dung beetles, the display case in which they have their home provides for their needs and is designed to show something of their extraordinary behaviour when it occurs. Nature wastes nothing and the dung beetle, as its name suggests, is an expert in collecting and using the droppings of larger, grazing animals as a food supply for their developing young. When collecting it, one or more of the insects will roll large balls of the dung to where they can use it. Seeing these tiny creatures manipulating such large quantities of matter – many times their own size – is a wonderful experience.

These creatures do much good in the wild, helping to clear away the dung so that the soil is not damaged by it and consequently the grass continues to grow well, providing plenty of food for the grazers which in their turn drop the dung that feeds the beetles. It's an excellent example of the natural cycle of life – even if it is difficult to spot on the way to the koalas!

GOING NATIVE

Nestled in the heart of the Highlands, 120 miles north of the city, there is an outpost of Edinburgh Zoo that cares for and shows off current and past Scottish native species; the Highland Wildlife Park at Kincraig in Inverness-shire. Here many of the amazing variety of native mammals, birds and reptiles that are found in present day Scotland live alongside rare animals that once were common, including some which are now extinct in Scotland

In a spectacular Highland setting in the Cairngorms National Park overlooking the river Spey, the animals roam free and visitors can see them from their cars as they drive around the reserve. This large conservation area contains some twenty five per cent of Britain's threatened birds, mammals and plants and the Wildlife Park naturally plays its part in ensuring that such animals and their habitats are properly conserved for future generations to appreciate and enjoy.

Opened in 1972, there is also a walk-round area that allows visitors to come close to some of the smaller species. The park was acquired by the Royal Zoological Society of Scotland in 1986.

The Highland Wildlife Park is divided into a number of habitats – forest, moorland, tundra, wetland and woodland. In addition there is an area for 'animals of the past', those species that have lived in the country, sometimes hundreds of thousand years ago, and have moved away or died out. For some, their previous life in Scotland can only be deduced from fossil remains; others were here more recently and are mentioned in historical records.

Not all of the animals that are in the park are kept in enclosures. There are many species that choose to live here – as they do in the park in Edinburgh.

Other wild animals have made their homes in and around the park, including small mammals such as the red squirrels (*Sciurus vulgaris*), rabbit (*Oryctolagus cuniculus*) and stoat (*Mustela erminea*). In summer, birds such as common buzzard (*Buteo buteo*), long-eared owl (*Asio otus*), lapwing (*Vanellus vanellus*), oystercatcher (*Haematopus ostralegus*), redshank (*Tringa totanus*) and snipe (*Gallinago gallinago*) all nest and rear their young in quieter corners.

There are many fenced-off areas for tree regeneration around the main reserve, where dozens of new deciduous trees are growing, including the aspen, which provide food for a multitude of insects, including twenty six moth species, the rarest being the dark-bordered beauty moth (*Epione vespertaria*).

The particular nature of the park reserve allows the visitor to be especially aware of the habitat of the animals. During the last Ice Age, some 11,000 years ago, this land lay beneath the glacier that eventually shaped the Spey Valley. Rocky outcrops and mounds of sand and gravel were left by the retreating ice, along

Previous page Red deer (IUCN staus: Least Concern)

with great boulders, known as 'erratics', and these can still be seen around the park. After the ice, the fertile earth encouraged the growth of trees and other flora that formed the rich habitat for the animals and birds.

The freshness and purity of the air is indicated by the clear presence of lichen that can be seen throughout the park on trees and rocks. Certain species of lichen will grow only where there is no pollution, showing that this is, indeed, a good place to live.

In the main reserve there are a number of species, large and small.

The mouflon (*Ovis musimon*) is a wild sheep that is thought to be one of the original ancestors of our modern domesticated variety. It can be found especially in mountainous areas above the tree line. Populations have recently been re-established into areas of Europe, but historically mouflon originated on the islands of Corsica, Sardinia and Cyprus.

The males and females live in separate groups for most of the year until the rut in late autumn and early winter. Then the rams reinforce their dominance hierarchy by crashing their horns together, resulting in older males and those with larger horns finally courting the females.

The ewes do not breed until they are two to three years old and the rams will not breed until they are around seven years old due to the need for a high social standing with the other males. How long a mouflon will live is directly linked to a herd's status. When the numbers in a population are stable or declining, most sheep will live over 10 years with a maximum life span of 20 years. In a growing population with heavy reproduction, the average life span is only six or seven years.

Mouflon have few natural predators, but in the wild they feed mostly at night and during daylight hours they can sit so still that it is possible to mistake them for a rock.

Soay sheep (*Ovis aries*) come, as their name suggests, from the island of Soay in the

Left Mouflon (IUCN status: Vulnerable)
Below Soay sheep (IUCN status: Not Listed)

windswept St Kilda group which lie to the west of the Outer Hebrides. With their soft woolly undercoat that was collected by the islanders and spun for weaving, this species is thought to be the only remaining example of the primitive sheep that were found in the British Isles before the coming of the Vikings and the Romans.

Another species useful to humans is the Highland cattle (*Bos taurus*). They are a hardy breed, well suited to life in the Scottish Highlands and Islands. Historically the predominant colour – especially on the islands – was black, but fashion in Victorian times led to the selective breeding of the lighter colours, giving us the now almost universal brownish/red animals. Originally this species was somewhat smaller than today and they were better able to survive on less winter-feeding than other breeds.

For centuries these cattle were an integral part of Scottish life, providing milk, meat, skins and even yarn from their long hair. The annual passages along the drove roads to markets in the south provide a colourful episode in many a historical narrative.

Above Red deer (IUCN staus: Least Concern)
Right European elk (IUCN staus: Least Concern)
Below Highland cattle (IUCN status: Not Listed)

It is thought that the cattle may have descended from the auroch or European wild ox, which was a native of Scotland from the last Ice Age to its extinction around the ninth century. The present animals still show more wild traits than their more domesticated cousins. For example, the cows are protective mothers and will often conceal their calves in the undergrowth for the first few days of their lives, returning only to feed them, much the same as red deer do.

The herd of red deer (*Cervus elaphus*) in the reserve are seen to have adapted well to the high open moorland. Traditionally a woodland creature, they lost out to the clearance of the forests for sheep farming.

The largest species of deer in Britain, the red deer's social life revolves around the female herd led by a leading hind. Those in the Highland Wildlife Park show all the dynamics of a wild herd and every season of the year brings different behaviours to the fore.

The impressive branched antlers of the males, used in season along with a characteristic strutting and bellowing to create or maintain dominance, are cast in the spring and new ones grow over a period of about three months, usually larger than the previous year. In the Scottish Highlands, stags chew on the old antlers when they break off. These bony antlers are rich in calcium, which is deficient in many soils of their habitat, and this vitamin source provides for future growth.

Red deer can be found in large numbers throughout Scotland, with calves being born in late May and June to take advantage of the better weather and living conditions.

Previously extinct in Scotland, the largest of the world's deer family, the European elk (*Alces alces alces*) was introduced into the reserve during 2005. Similar to the subspecies known in North America as moose (*Alces alces americanus*), this animal became extinct here in

Britain due to climate change in the period 3,000 to 7,000 years ago.

A fully-grown bull elk can stand over two metres high at the shoulders and has large palmate antlers (shaped like an open hand), which weigh up to 20 kilograms. Their often ungainly-looking long legs are designed for speed and endurance and, besides being excellent swimmers, they can gallop at up to 60 kilometres per hour, a useful skill when they want to escape predators such as wolves, lynx and brown bear.

Adult elk live a mainly solitary life for most of the year, although females do sometimes form very small groups. The three elk in the park came from Kolmarden Zoo in Sweden and are currently the only elk of any sub species in the British Isles.

The arrival of the elk meant that one of the longer-established species had to be moved within the reserve. The Przewalski's stallion became very aggressive towards them, leading to the horse herd being moved away to avoid conflict.

Believed to be extinct in the wild, Przewalski's horse (*Equus caballus przewalskii*) was discovered and identified in the late nineteenth century by the Russian explorer, Nicolai Przhevalsky. These are the only true living wild horses. All the animals alive today are direct descendants of the small population, which had been taken into zoos throughout the world at the start of the twentieth century. By 1945 there were very few animals left. In order to prevent inbreeding, carefully monitored exchanges were encouraged between zoos and the population is now in the hundreds.

Their presence in Scotland is indicated by fossil evidence, which suggests that wild horses survived in the region until about 3,000 years ago. European Neolithic cave paintings are another source of evidence for the existence of this species this far west. The last wild population was found in Mongolia and the Przewalski's horse is presently being reintroduced into two main sites in Mongolia where herds have re-established themselves well. They provide an excellent example of just how effective co-ordinated conservation programmes managed by zoos can be.

The stocky, short-legged Przewalski's horses differ from domestic horses in a number of ways. Their skull is heavier and they have a thicker jaw as well as an upright black mane and no forelock in contrast to their yellowish brown body coat with black lower legs and a black tail. Their coat grows very thick and woolly in winter.

Foals have been born in the park and thus, once again, the Royal Zoological Society of Scotland is continuing to play an important part in the survival of another very rare species of animal.

Another animal that has come from other parts of Europe is the European bison (*Bison bonasus*). It is this continent's largest land mammal and has been extinct over most of its range in the wild since prehistoric times. Surviving numbers in Poland, Russia, Belarus and the Ukraine were hunted heavily in the nineteenth century and taken in vast numbers for food by troops during the First World War.

The last wild-roaming bison was shot in Bialowieza forest in Poland in 1919. Almost immediately, however, a captive breeding programme was started with the remaining zoo animals. By the middle of the twentieth century there were about 120 animals surviving and some were returned to their central European native habitat.

With some 3,500 animals of this species living worldwide – all of which descended

Left Przewalski's horse
(IUCN status: Extinct in the Wild)

from just 12 individuals, it is not surprising that there are problems associated with inbreeding. Careful monitoring and breeding recommendations from the European bison studbook holder ensures that such problems are kept to a minimum and a healthy and secure population survives.

All of the Highland Wildlife Park's bison are part of the international breeding programme and it currently has the largest herd of European bison in the United Kingdom.

Less muscular but taller than the American bison, European bison prefer a woodland habitat where they live in small herds, browsing on leaves and vegetation. Most of the year the cows and calves will form a herd, which will be joined by bulls around July, leading up to the rut in August and October.

European bison are mainly grazers and they can spend up to sixty per cent of daylight

Left European bison (IUCN status: Endangered)

Below Wolf (IUCN status: Least Concern)

hours feeding. They do not have any natural predators in the areas where they roam. This fact, coupled with abundant food supplies means that there is a very small mortality rate, so the future is positive for these huge animals.

There were some reports in the last century of some bison being attacked by wolves (though they probably now go for more easily caught prey such as deer), and the wolf enclosure within the park is a popular one.

The wolf (*Canis lupus*) is an intelligent and social animal that is believed to have become extinct in Scotland when the last one was shot in 1743, and it is now vulnerable in parts of its range across Europe. Here in the Wildlife Park there is a pack that functions well within its well-organised social hierarchy and it is interesting to look for examples of this. If the tail is held high, then it is probably the leader, the alpha male.

An ancestor of the domestic dog, this pack animal can hunt and kill a prey as much as ten times its own weight.

The Arctic fox (*Alopex lagopus*), a similarly social animal, would have been found following the wolf packs and reindeer herds during the Ice Age, scavenging for leftovers to supplement their diet of lemmings. Their short greyish fur of the summer turns into a thick white thermal coat when the cold of winter sets in.

The lynx (*Lynx lynx*) is Europe's largest cat and a powerful hunter, preying on mammals and even birds that they can flush out and catch in mid-air.

Much persecuted by farmers because they will take livestock, as well as being frequent victims of road-kill, the Eurasian lynx seems also to suffer from a mysterious loss of male cubs in the wild. It is thought that this may be due to a genetic problem, so their carefully managed presence in the park is of particular relevance and importance.

The succulence of its meat and the thrill of the chase have meant that the wild boar (*Sus scrofa*) stood little chance of remaining in Scotland. The loss of its natural habitat also helped in its decline. Still quite widespread throughout the rest of Europe, the wild boar can be quite aggressive when alarmed – especially the males with their sharp tusks and great agility.

Large herds of reindeer (*Rangifer tarandus*) once roamed over Scotland, but now they are found in the wild only in much more northern countries. Here they are known to travel extensively – up to 40 miles in a day, but the animals in the park do not have to go quite so far to meet all of their physical needs.

Many of the other animals within the Highland Wildlife Park are still found in wild places throughout the country, but visitors are able to see them all within a comparatively small space, thriving and being healthy ambassadors for their less visible fellows.

Below Arctic fox (IUCN staus: Least Concern)

Below Wild boar (IUCN staus: Lower Risk)

Above Reindeer (IUCN staus: Lower Risk)

Right Polecat (IUCN staus: Lower Risk)

The richest variety of wildlife still exists in the remnants of the ancient Caledonian forest. Happily there is a real will to regenerate and restore this wonderful habitat and so there is a slow increase in places for the animals to live.

Animals from this forest habitat and found within the park include the polecat (*Mustela putorius*), a wild relative of the domestic ferret. If threatened, it lets off a pungent-smelling secretion and, along with the smell, can be recognised by its distinctive 'robber's mask'.

The pine marten (*Martes martes*), sometimes known as the 'tree weasel', is well adapted for life above the ground. Both of the animals in the park are wild-born. They were found as orphans and hand-reared by keepers.

In Scotland they like to live in open pine forest, chiefly in Grampian and the Highlands where they can nest in tree holes or a former squirrel drey. Historically, they were persecuted for their fur and by gamekeepers, so much so that by 1926 the main population was restricted to a small area of north-west Scotland. They are very shy creatures but are now increasing in some areas of Scotland due to increased forestry and enlightened estate management, which can provide plenty of food, including voles, squirrels and other small mammals along with birds and even berries.

It is to be hoped that the pine marten does not particularly persecute the native red squirrel over its more common grey cousin.

There are about 246 different species of squirrel throughout the world, but the only one native to Britain is the European red squirrel (*Sciurus vulgaris*). They are very rare now, living mainly in small pockets of conifer woodland in Scotland. Up to a dozen free-ranging red squirrels regularly visit the feeding stations provided in the forest habitat section of the park.

The grey squirrel (*Sciurus carolinensis*) was once a zoo animal itself, introduced for comparison with our native species from North America. Thought originally to have adapted well, some of these animals were allowed to roam free and it was not long before they became the dominant group, forcing out the natives.

Such history has led to a more informed management of introduced animals to ensure that similar things do not happen to other species.

The wildcat (*Felis silvestris*) is very like our pet cat and, indeed, the main threat to its pure existence these days is the likelihood of its interbreeding with feral domestic animals. It is slightly larger and heavier with a longer coat than its domestic tabby cousin.

Another species that is causing much discussion about the possibility of its reintroduction into the wild in this country is the European beaver (*Castor fiber*). The continent's largest rodent, beavers are seen as nature's hardest workers. It is this that seems to disturb some people!

Beavers spend most of their time in or near water and, in order to regulate the depth of water to their needs, they often build spectacular and effective dams. Strong front teeth enable them to cut down trees up to a metre in diameter. These are then used to make the dam that ensures that the entrance to their home, called a lodge, is safely under water.

Those in the park came from Bavaria in south Germany and they are no exception to the rule, having constructed a complex system of tunnels in the bank. Some of the birch trees around their enclosure have had to be fenced off to protect them from the beaver's activity.

Some people believe that these activities harm crops and trees and affect other local wildlife. Others think that it is more likely that they help to reduce local floods and to return the habitat to its more natural state. Six beavers were reintroduced into Gloucestershire in October 2005 so it will be interesting to see how this develops.

The European otter (*Lutra lutra*) is another species that is well adapted to its semi-aquatic life. Otters are members of the same family as the badger and stoat – the mustelids – but have adapted to life in the water.

Left Wildcat (IUCN status: Vulnerable)

Below left European beaver
(IUCN status: Near Threatened)

Below right European otter
(IUCN status: Near Threatened)

A generally secretive animal, it tends to be nocturnal, but in more remote areas it is active during the day. Populations of otter can be found in Europe, Scandinavia, most of the former USSR and North Africa. The coasts around Scotland and Ireland are where the species is mostly found in the British Isles, however they are increasingly being found in more urban areas thanks to the return of fish to our less polluted rivers.

The Highland Wildlife Park otters enjoy their 'Brightwater Burn' enclosure, named after Gavin Maxwell's account of his experience of two otters in 'Ring of Bright Water', published in 1960 and made famous by the film with the same title in 1969.

Wetlands, found where water meets the land, are very important habitats, supporting a complete range from micro-organisms to large mammals. They provide winter feeding and summer breeding grounds, but are greatly under threat from land drainage and pollution. Just below the park – and visible from the lookout area – is probably the most important wetland site in Scotland, the Insh Marshes, parts of which have been designated an RSPB National Nature Reserve.

Another suitable stretch of water plays a huge part in attracting a variety of wildfowl and that is the lochan by the park's visitor centre. Visitors, including greylag, barnacle, white-fronted and pink-footed geese and pintail, tufted and goldeneye ducks can outnumber the residents here at certain times of the year.

Lovers of birds will find much to attract them within the park; from calling waders and hooting eagle owls to popping capercaillie and red or black grouse noisily displaying.

The vivarium, representing the source of a river with its mossy banks and trickling water, also caters for particular tastes. It contains three native species of slow worm, common lizard and palmate newt.

Careful management of the land, such as regular burning by man and grazing by animals halts the natural re-growth of trees on the moorland and it can be seen that this habitat supports some unique species of wildlife. Above 600 metres, heather gives way to alpine plants. On the tops of the Cairngorms, on bare damp ground, sedges, grasses, dwarf willow, dwarf birches and mosses all play their part in the creation of a tundra habitat, with its particular wildlife.

Much of the main reserve only fifty years ago would have been given over to broadleaf woodlands. Today only a fragment of Scotland's broadleaf woodland remains, yet the park can offer some of it – helping to support the variety of animals that are cared for here.

The Highland Wildlife Park, in its spectacular setting, offers something of everything, and something for everyone. Forest habitat gives way to woodland, tundra to moorland, and moorland to wetland. Perhaps more than anywhere else, this is the place to come to experience and enjoy the changing times and seasons: from bitter snowy winter, that is no problem for the European bison, through spring and the casting of the red deer antlers and the arrival of the wading birds; from summer and the birth of the first young, through autumn and the great male battles for dominance; this is the place to be.

Capercaillie (IUCN staus: Least Concern)

LOOKING
TO THE
FUTURE

The Royal Zoological Society of Scotland that is responsible for the running of Edinburgh Zoo and the Highland Wildlife Park has a great plan for development in the coming years.

With the one-hundredth anniversary of the founding of the zoo coming up, a £58 million redevelopment project has been launched and is underway. True to the vision of the Society's founders, and accelerating the positive changes seen over recent years, it will create a world-class visitor attraction and a conservation centre of excellence.

Changes will allow visitors to immerse themselves even more fully in a natural environment where they can see rare and exciting animals in a modern, attractive setting.

Much will be done to improve the comfort of both the animals and the visitors.

On the understanding that habitat is crucial to species conservation, the new zoo will include four major biomes: Oceans & Wetlands, Grasslands, Tropical Forest and Woodlands, each of which represents a

---

Previous page Gelada baboon
(IUCN status: Near Threatened)

Below An artist's impression of one of the options for the entrance complex

different habitat around the world. In addition, a Scottish Conservation Area will be developed to the east of the current site.

A brand new modern public entrance will be built at the top of the existing car park. It is designed to give immediate access to three of the four biomes and will feature a large, open plaza that will enable visitors to get their bearings. An environmentally-friendly transport system will offer motorised travel around the biomes for all visitors, especially welcome for those with mobility problems and families with small children.

The park itself will have to be redeveloped and all of the building work carried out while the zoo is still open to the public and much careful thought and planning is going on to ensure that disruption to the animals and the visitors is kept to a minimum. Fortunately the nature of the site is such that it should be quite possible to isolate the building areas until they are ready for occupation and available to the visitors.

In harmony with the new biomes, the best features of the current set up will be retained, improved or added to. The use of high level walkways, dense planting, natural materials and running water will continue to provide a truly atmospheric feel for the visitor. The natural rock

and mature trees in the park will no doubt provide a dramatic backdrop for these exhibits.

The biomes themselves will house an animal collection of which at least seventy per cent will be endangered species. Many of the popular animals will remain, but there will be more mixed exhibits with fewer barriers and more natural settings. In many cases, where the needs of the animals allow, visitors will be able to share the same space as the animals, enabling them to feel truly immersed in the experience.

Below An impression of the proposed redevelopment of the Mansion House

The Tropical Forest Biome in the east of the park will contain the 'Living Links' primate study centre and the new Budongo Forest exhibit. This exciting new exhibit will be an entirely new concept in animal enclosure, largely based on an area of rainforest in Uganda that the Society is managing for conservation. Chimpanzees will have a number of different living spaces, connected by tunnels, so that they can move around as they would through forest corridors, and can remain on their own or mix with others, as they choose.

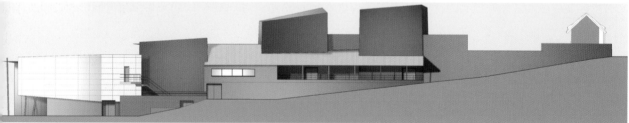

The Oceans and Wetlands Biome will include a large aquatic area for manatees, turtles, pygmy hippos and other tropical species. It is planned to link this beautiful area to dining and corporate hospitality areas, allowing underwater viewing along one whole wall of the restaurant.

The current penguin pool, which even now, being in its second decade, remains one of the best such enclosures in the world, will be kept and quietly developed.

At the top of the park will be the Grassland Biome. Here the wide, relatively flat and open topography will enable the provision of superb spaces for giraffes, Indian rhinos and gelada baboons. The fabulous views over the city of Edinburgh will be seen by even more people as they enjoy this newly laid out area at the top of the hill. The design of this biome will enable visitors truly to get close to these magnificent animals.

Left The Budongo Forest exhibit showing sections through the south, east and west elevations

Below An impression of the Tropical Forest biome

The Woodland Biome will retain most of the existing trees and topography in the centre of the zoo park, with lions and tigers continuing to be the main animals featured. The hillside nature of this section splendidly allows for the building out of viewing platforms, giving an excellent view of some of the animals without disturbing them. It may also see the return of elephants to Edinburgh for the first time since the 1980s.

In tandem with all the physical re-development of the park over the next twenty years, the Society is seeking to demonstrate and communicate more fully its aims and the important work it is doing. The new habitats will enable it to do so in ways which will excite and engage the visitors.

All of these redevelopments and the constantly changing needs of the animals mean that visitors will experience an ever-changing collection. Individual animals and species will come and go over the years. Being a responsible, modern zoo, part of an international network of conservation programmes, it has a duty to respond to the needs of threatened species as

these programmes identify them. Consequently some of the plans may be altered over the years, but only in line with species conservation and the best animal welfare.

As might be expected, much thought has gone into the principles behind all of the planned changes. Demonstrating its commitment to sustainable development, the Society will ensure that all of the work and provision for the animals and humans will be as environmentally sustainable as possible. A new borehole has been dug and is expected to provide most of the water required by the site. Efficient use of water through recycling, rainwater collection and reed bed filtration will continue and be developed.

Renewable energy options are being investigated, such as solar and wind power and ground heat pumps. Energy efficiency will be a key component of building design and materials. Advantage will be taken of the latest technology such as smart systems to minimise energy use. It will, indeed, be a brave new world.

In developing the park to make it generally more attractive, much of the current planting; mature trees, shrubs and plants, will be retained. The natural biodiversity of the site will be protected and, if anything, improved.

Other plans for the future include the setting up and running of outposts elsewhere in Scotland and working in co-operation with a variety of other bodies, such as governmental organisations and charities with an interest in wildlife, along with museums and educational establishments, to give a more rounded picture and access to the zoo's animal collection and its conservation work.

The opening of the 'Living Links' centre within the zoo park being run jointly with universities for purposes of observational research is, of course, another aspect of this same desire to open out the work in many new and innovative ways.

In the meantime, the zoo does not stand still. Regular visitors immediately can see that the place is in a continual state of change for the better. Animals are moved into different areas or in and out of the zoo altogether, depending on their needs. It may be that a new enriched enclosure will be provided. Thus the giraffes are sent off to another zoo in Denmark where they are playing an important part in the breeding programme for their species as well as delighting a completely new

Below An impression of the Oceans and Wetlands biome featuring spectacular underwater viewing

set of visitors. Meanwhile, their previous enclosure is developed for the benefit of another species.

Zoo staff at all levels are encouraged to study, attend conferences and to travel to other places in order to share their expertise and to learn more about the keeping of animals. A successful new style of building or enclosure seen elsewhere can be adapted for use in Edinburgh once the team is convinced that the principles are sound. With a strong senior management team, backed by an enthusiastic and knowledgeable council, the zoo staff can offer most of the necessary skills for providing regular new and improved habitats for the best care of the animals.

Below The Grasslands node, with interpretation and retail, catering and play opportunities on a 'grassland' theme

The visitors, part of the lifeblood of the zoo, are not left out. Its place as the second most visited paying attraction in Scotland – after Edinburgh Castle – means that the zoo must constantly be looking at what it offers by way of the quality of visitor experience.

When even the lavatories have won an award then it can be seen that every aspect is taken seriously. Once again, regular visitors will find that nothing stands still. Every visit to the shop will reveal new items, menus in the various food outlets are continuously changing to provide both old favourites and new meals, with healthy options and organic ingredients, to tempt the palate of the visitors who don't bring their own picnics.

The events team are tirelessly working with all of the staff to come up with interesting ideas that will attract visitors old and new. An African themed evening, for example, might involve keeper talks about the chosen continent and the animals from there that are found in the zoo park, along with music and dance, food and entertainment, all with an African flavour. As well as the talks, there may

also be literature available on the day to tell the story of conservation work being done *in situ*. It is a team effort that takes much planning and is hard work for all, but seeing hundreds of people leaving at the end of a successful evening is its own reward. The fact that they may have left with a deeper understanding of, and appreciation for, the conservation of endangered species in Africa, is the added bonus which demonstrates the power of zoos to make a difference.

The interpretation officer, a skilled communicator, works with all of the staff – from those on the front reception desk to the keepers, volunteers and education staff – to ensure that there is constantly evolving material to enhance understanding of what the visitor is seeing around the zoo park. This might be a simple explanation about why an animal is behaving in a particular way, perhaps to do with mating rituals or veterinary treatment, to clear maps showing the natural range of a species and telling of its current status in the wild, or some fascinating aspect of its behaviour or social structure.

Below An impression of the Woodlands biome

The education department, working with people of all ages, constantly looks for ways in which the stories of biodiversity and conservation can be told. Animals and their welfare, research into their needs and behaviours, conservation measures being undertaken in their natural wild habitats all need talking about. Aiming fully to engage those with whom they come into contact, much of the education work is exciting and innovative – well beyond the natural excitement of any primary class seeing wild animals for the first time in their young lives.

Projects such as the Global Classroom that will bring together young people from all over the world, thanks to satellite technology, are just one example of this.

Senior staff, often involved mostly in administration, along with members of the zoo's governing body, work behind the scenes to find ways that will improve the lot of the animals in both the zoo and the wild. The business of fundraising may seem dull to some, but it is a vital part of the work of the Society, enabling it to fund many important projects at home and overseas to secure the future of the great diversity of wildlife and habitats with which they are linked.

The Royal Zoological Society of Scotland, Edinburgh Zoo and the Highland Wildlife Park do not exist in isolation and much representative work will continue. Those with particular skills may sit on committees, perhaps for local or national government, or serve national and international professional bodies in a variety of ways. Staff may also pass on some of their own observations and experience through papers to conferences of fellow workers in the field.

A regular output of literature like the seasonal park map, members' magazines and an annual report must be written, designed and distributed.

With much general public interest in the zoo and nearly 20,000 members, both external and internal communications are hugely important. The media is always interested in the birth of unusual and often rare babies that will increase and enhance the global population of a species. Equally it is sometimes necessary and important publicly to face animal rights advocates who find the very existence of zoos disagreeable. Different ideas and perspectives should be openly debated and the Society is always willing to hold its head high and tell of the excellence of the work it does on behalf of the world's wildlife.

These are exciting times for all concerned with and interested in Edinburgh Zoo. A much-loved place that seems to be owned by all Scots and proudly shown off to visitors to the city, the park and its collection of animals undoubtedly will continue to thrive and do much for the good of animals and peoples throughout the world.

Despite all the everyday things described, the zoo really has one absolute and central reason for its being, and aim for its work. The conservation of the rich heritage of the natural world and the many threatened species of animals must always be at the centre of all that it does. Throughout the world there is a growing and general consensus that zoos play an increasingly necessary and vital role in this great task.

The World Association of Zoos and Aquariums (WAZA), based in Switzerland, brings together zoos and aquariums from across the globe and helps them all to define the necessary standards, practices and policies that might help achieve conservation goals. It makes the point that zoos are in a unique position to provide conservation in a genuinely integrated way.

A zoo like Edinburgh is often the first dramatic point of contact with the wonderful world of nature that a young person may have.

Plan of the zoo before the new developments

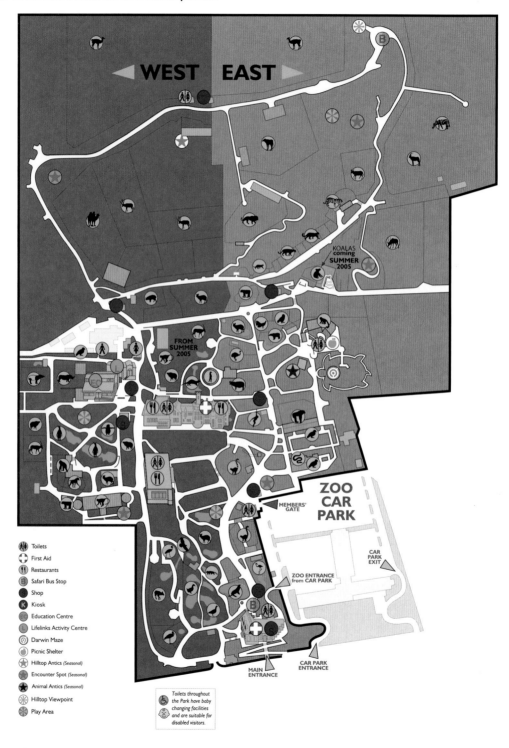

WEST   EAST

KOALAS
coming
SUMMER
2005

FROM
SUMMER
2005

ZOO
CAR
PARK

MEMBERS'
GATE

CAR
PARK
EXIT

ZOO ENTRANCE
from CAR PARK

CAR PARK
ENTRANCE

MAIN
ENTRANCE

- Toilets
- First Aid
- Restaurants
- Safari Bus Stop
- Shop
- Kiosk
- Education Centre
- Lifelinks Activity Centre
- Darwin Maze
- Picnic Shelter
- Hilltop Antics *(Seasonal)*
- Encounter Spot *(Seasonal)*
- Animal Antics *(Seasonal)*
- Hilltop Viewpoint
- Play Area

Toilets throughout
the Park have baby
changing facilities
and are suitable for
disabled visitors.

Proposed plan of new zoo, featuring habitat biomes, transport system and new Scottish conservation area

The director general of IUCN, the World Conservation Union, suggests that this makes the zoo 'the incubator of the conservationists of tomorrow'.

'The research that is conducted in and by the zoo is 'vital to our understanding of the components of biodiversity and their interactions'.

The public awareness campaigns and communication of the zoo's message 'are critical in making the general public understand both the utilitarian and the aesthetic importance of nature'.

The sheer scale of the practical welfare programme for the animals and the continuing transfer of ideas and technology between zoos throughout the world is also seen as an essential contribution to biodiversity conservation as well as contributing to a true spirit of collaboration and co-operation in a troubled world.

Media reporting of human and natural disasters, from the violence of war and the appalling consequences of famine to drought and flood, mean that we are all much more aware than we have ever been about the interconnections between people and the fragility of the natural world. Awareness, however, does not mean understanding, and it is often necessary to point out that many of the terrible consequences of these crises could have been avoided.

The importance and value of preserving the natural balance of biodiversity and our ecosystems, despite the demands of human development and progress, cannot be stressed enough. But we are selfish and sometimes short-sighted. Zoos, through their good work, can help us to see more clearly the needs of a natural world under siege. The negative influence that humankind is having on habitats, and the fauna and flora with which we share our world and which ultimately help us to maintain it, must be overcome.

Every individual zoo can help, as long as it is properly managed and sincerely committed to the aim. In fact, it could be argued that it is supremely suited for the task.

It is no accident that the Royal Zoological Society of Scotland emphasises its global approach. Science has told us of the interconnections of all life systems and the importance of maintaining habitats. In the zoo and wildlife park there is a long established body of knowledge and expertise in the care of collections of living animals from all over the world. The Society is part of a well functioning and effective global network.

The zoo can and does operate over the complete spectrum of conservation activities. It cares for and breeds threatened species. It is involved in public education, training and advocacy. It provides for scientific research within the zoo. But that is not all. Internationally it works *in situ*, supporting particular threatened species and their habitats and working with local people to this end.

The hundreds of thousands of visitors that come through the gates every year are to an extent a 'captive audience' for participating in this integrated approach. Given knowledge and understanding, they too can be positively influenced and may even become ambassadors and advocates themselves. Such a body of people on side can be a real force for social and political change.

Models of 'integrated conservation', zoos through their work and their supporters really can make a true difference to our planet and all of the life that it sustains. In the future there is no doubt that the definitions and boundaries will blur. No longer will any aspect of the work be seen in isolation.

Already this is seen in Edinburgh as keepers leave their day-to-day work to spend time overseas, working with similar animals in the wild. The scientific community is moving some of its work directly into the zoo, as seen with the primate study centre. The vision of the early founders of the zoo is being realised in new and different ways.

Always in the forefront of animal welfare, education, research and conservation, the future plans are designed to push the boundaries even further.

As the future plans take shape, the dynamic place that Edinburgh zoo is now will be even more amongst the world's leaders in these fields, a shining example of all that is excellent in integrated conservation.

Index

Page numbers in *italics* refer to illustrations

CONTACTS

The Royal Zoological Society of Scotland
Edinburgh Zoo
Corstorphine Road
Edinburgh EH12 6TS
0131-334 9171
info@rzss.org.uk
www.edinburghzoo.org.uk

The Royal Zoological Society of Scotland
Highland Wildlife Park
Kincraig
Kingussie PH21 1NL
01540 651270
info@highlandwildlifepark.org
www.highlandwildlifepark.org

Charity no. SC 004064